To Mary Ellen Rutter—

Bon Appétit!

The Happy Camper's Gourmet Cookbook

Joyce Ryan

BUTTERFLY
B O O K S

Published by Butterfly Books
4210 Misty Glade
San Antonio, Texas 78247

Tel. 512-494-0077

Manufactured in the United States of America

Printed by McNaughton & Gunn, Inc.
960 Woodland Drive
Saline, Michigan 48176

Camera work by Jimgraphics
7950 Mainland
San Antonio, Texas 78250

Library of Congress Cataloging-in-Publication Data

Ryan, Joyce E.
   The Happy Camper's Gourmet Cookbook
   Bibliography:p.
   Includes index
   1. Cookery. I. Title.
Library of Congress Number: 92-70449

ISBN 0-939077-03-5

Dedication

To Mother, the best cook in the world, for teaching me how to cook and instilling in me the desire to excel.

Also by Joyce Ryan

Traveling with your Sketchbook
Seoul Travel Guide
Scenes of Southern Arizona
Seoul Sketches

ACKNOWLEDGMENTS

I extend sincere gratitude to Priscilla Grijalva
and Sharon Hoelscher Day for their generosity in
supplying technical information. Heartfelt thanks to
Zora Baker, Melba Specht, and Frank Thomas who
cheerfully and tactfully tasted my recipes. I am also
indebted to Mark Johnson for his beautiful photographs.
Special thanks to Jim Klar for his helpful criticism and
professional advice.

For permission to include a table regarding high altitude
baking: Cooperative Extension Service of New Mexico
State University.

CONTENTS

Introduction

Basic Pantry 10

Equipment 18

Loading your Camper/RV 22

Appetizers 25

Beverages 39

Breads 44

Main Dishes 60

Side Dishes 127

Desserts 150

Menus 174

Coping with Problems 180

Substitutions/Equivalents 184

Bibliography 188
Index 189
About the Author

INTRODUCTION

A traveling gourmet is a special cook. That person finds the exhilarating experience of visiting new places as enjoyable as preparing a delicious meal. But cooking while traveling requires exceptional skill. While campers and recreational vehicles can offer many of the conveniences of a modern kitchen, restricted space makes food preparation, cooking, and storage difficult. Planning is essential.

Traveling throughout the United States presents additional challenges. Coping with the arid desert of Arizona, the high altitude of Colorado, and the damp, humid climate of Louisiana can prove vexing to even the most experienced chef.

This cookbook provides practical information and thoroughly tested recipes that will help you successfully combine your love of traveling and your love of cooking. Learn how to efficiently equip your camper, stock your pantry, plan menus, and deal with the perplexing problems of humidity, high altitude, and extreme dryness. And, I hope the 248 delicious recipes will tempt your taste buds and stimulate your appetite.

BON VOYAGE and BON APPÉTIT

Joyce Ryan

BASIC PANTRY

Your pantry while camping does not have to be skimpy or inadequate due to limited space. An incredible variety of ingredients will fit in your camper if you repackage items into smaller containers. Thoughtful planning will enable you to make room for many of your special ingredients.

SELECTION OF ITEMS

The basic pantry should consist of items that are frequently used. Expand the basic pantry by packing anticipated quantities of seldom used items in small containers for special recipes that you have planned. Following this simple logic when stocking your supplies will enable you to make the best use of the available space.

An extensive master supply list begins on page 12. Read through the list slowly, then select items critical to your cooking. Start by including all the items that you feel are essential; then as you actually stock your camper, place the less important items in small containers. Obviously, space restrictions will require some items to be eliminated.

A basic pantry is a very personal affair. I am including my personal list for your reference (see pages 16,17). As you read my list, you will want to eliminate some items and add others.

A quick glance at my list demonstrates how much I like to bake. If you are an occasional baker or your camper does not have an oven, obviously many of those items will be eliminated.

QUANTITIES

Determine the quantities of needed items by how often you use them and the amount generally used. For example, canned tomatoes are a frequently used ingredient in my cooking. For a two week trip I take three 1-lb. cans. Shortening is another essential item. I use only small amounts, so I typically pack 1/2 cup in a small plastic container.

The length of your trip is another factor when deciding quantity. Normally I stock my pantry with one can each of tuna, crab, and clams. However, on a six-month trip to Alaska, I had an entire crate of canned fish.

Consider stocking large quantities of dry goods for long trips. Foods with a long shelf life such as rice and pasta are convenient, inexpensive, and healthy additions to your stock/pantry.

When traveling in Canada, you will discover that most American cooking ingredients (even the same brand) are available. All items are metrically packaged which can be confusing when trying to follow American recipes (see page 187 for metric equivalents). I prefer to pack extra canned goods to avoid the hassle of metric conversion. The Canadian products are also more expensive.

ORGANIZATION OF PANTRY LIST

Organize your pantry list according to where you store the items. This makes restocking your supplies much easier. Typical storage areas include refrigerator, freezer, cabinets, drawers, and storage boxes/crates.

LOCATION OF LIST

Tape a copy of your basic pantry list inside a cabinet or other convenient location. Having it readily available makes assessment of your stock before and during the trip a snap.

REVALUATION OF LIST

Re-evaluate your basic pantry after a major trip. Most assuredly there will be items taking up valuable space that just are not as important as you originally thought. Additions to your list are also likely.

MASTER SHOPPING/SUPPLY LIST

Prepare a personalized list by reviewing the following items.

PASTA, GRAINS, CEREAL
__breakfast cereals
__oatmeal
__spaghetti
__macaroni
__manicotti
__lasagne
__egg noodles
__rice
__wild rice
__popcorn
__chips

DAIRY
__milk
__cream
__half-and-half
__sour cream
__yogurt
__butter
__margarine
__cream cheese
__cheese
__eggs

BEVERAGES
__nonfat dry milk
__coffee
__tea
__dry creamer
__instant orange juice
__soda
__wine
__beer
__liquor
__liqueur

FROZEN
__orange juice
__pie shells
__bread dough
__vegetables
__fruits
__non-dairy whipped topping
__ice cream

CANNED MEAT/FISH
__tuna
__salmon
__crab
__clam
__oysters
__anchovy
__shrimp
__chicken

GELATINS
__unflavored
__flavored

BAKING/STAPLES
__flour
__self-rising flour
__wheat flour
__corn meal
__biscuit mix
__cornstarch
__Italian bread crumbs
__sugar
__confectioners' sugar
__brown sugar
__cocoa
__unsweetened chocolate
__semisweet chocolate
__sweet chocolate
__chocolate chips
__sweetened condensed milk
__evaporated milk
__vegetable oil
__shortening
__vegetable cooking spray
__baking soda
__baking powder
__yeast
__vanilla extract
__almond extract
__nuts
__salt
__coarse black pepper
__spices & herbs

13

CONDIMENTS
__mayonnaise
__salad dressing
__ragù sauce
__BBQ sauce
__yellow mustard
__Dijon mustard
__horseradish
__vinegar
__cider vinegar
__wine vinegar
__Worcestershire sauce
__steak sauce
__soy sauce
__capers
__pickles
__green olives
__black olives
__green chilies
__tomato paste
__tomato sauce
__tomato soup
__cream of mushroom soup
__cream of chicken soup
__chicken bouillon
__beef bouillon
__consommé
__honey
__jam/jelly
__corn syrup
__molasses
__pancake syrup
__peanut butter

PRODUCE
__apples
__bananas
__lemons
__lettuce
__green onion
__radish
__carrots
__green pepper
__cauliflower
__broccoli
__zucchini
__potatoes
__onions
__garlic
__other

MEAT/FISH
__chicken
__beef
__ground beef
__ham
__bacon
__pork
__turkey
__lamb
__veal
__fish
__shrimp
__luncheon meats
__sausage

CANNED AND DRIED VEGETABLES/FRUITS
__tomatoes
__pork and beans
__refried beans
__kidney beans
__navy beans
__green beans
__beets
__peas
__cream style corn
__whole kernel corn
__mushrooms
__raisins
__dates
__prunes
__apricots
__maraschino cherries
__blueberries

BAKERY
__bread
__rolls
__crackers
__cookies

KITCHEN CLEANSERS
__dishwashing liquid
__sponges
__scouring pads
__spray cleanser/abrasive
  cleanser
__pot scrubber

KITCHEN SUPPLIES
__coffee filters
__napkins
__aluminum foil
__wax paper
__plastic wrap
__gallon plastic storage
  bags & ties
__sandwich bags
__garbage bags & ties
__paper plates
__paper cups
__toothpicks
__plastic knives, forks,
  & spoons

ADDITIONAL SUPPLIES
__paper towels
__toilet tissue
__furniture polish
__glass cleaner
__laundry detergent
__spot remover
__matches
__butane lighter
__charcoal lighter fluid
__charcoal
__first aid kit
__fire extinguisher

MY BASIC SHOPPING/SUPPLY LIST
My list is organized according to where items are stored.

BAKING/STAPLES
__ flour
__ wheat flour
__ biscuit mix
__ corn meal
__ Italian bread crumbs
__ cornstarch
__ sugar
__ brown sugar
__ confectioners' sugar
__ baking soda
__ baking powder
__ yeast
__ semisweet chocolate
__ chocolate chips
__ evaporated milk
__ sweetened condensed milk
__ vanilla extract
__ almond extract
__ vegetable oil
__ shortening
__ vegetable cooking spray
__ chopped nuts
__ salt
__ coarse black pepper
__ spices & herbs

GRAINS
__ rice
__ wild rice
__ spaghetti
__ macaroni
__ breakfast cereals
__ oatmeal
__ bread

SNACKS
__ graham crackers
__ crackers
__ popcorn
__ raisins
__ peanut butter
__ honey

CANNED FOOD
__ tomatoes
__ peas
__ cream style corn
__ refried beans
__ pork and beans
__ sliced mushrooms
__ black olives
__ green olives
__ green chilies
__ cream of mushroom soup
__ cream of potato soup
__ chicken bouillon cubes
__ instant chicken bouillon
__ tomato sauce
__ tomato paste
__ Italian dressing packages
__ vinegar
__ tuna
__ crab
__ clam

BEVERAGES
__ sodas
__ coffee
__ instant orange juice
__ nonfat dry milk
__ instant coffee
__ dry creamer
__ liqueur
__ liquor
__ sherry
__ wine

PRODUCE (NONREFRIGERATED)
__ potatoes
__ onions
__ banana

REFRIGERATED ITEMS
_ milk
_ butter/margarine
_ eggs
_ cheese
_ Parmesan cheese
_ cream cheese
_ salad dressings
_ yogurt
_ catsup
_ Dijon mustard
_ yellow mustard
_ mayonnaise
_ Worcestershire sauce
_ steak sauce
_ soy sauce
_ lemon juice
_ jam/jelly
_ horseradish
_ fruit
_ lettuce
_ carrots
_ green onion
_ cauliflower
_ broccoli
_ radish
_ garlic

FREEZER ITEMS
_ orange juice
_ chopped green pepper
_ smoked sausage
_ chicken breasts
_ steak
_ ground beef
_ peas
_ green beans

KITCHEN CLEANSERS
_ dishwashing liquid
_ sponges
_ scouring pads
_ spray cleanser/abrasive cleanser
_ pot scrubber

KITCHEN SUPPLIES
_ coffee filters
_ napkins
_ aluminum foil
_ wax paper
_ plastic wrap
_ gallon plastic storage
  bags & ties
_ sandwich bags
_ garbage bags & ties
_ paper plates
_ paper cups
_ toothpicks
_ plastic knives, forks,
  & spoons

ADDITIONAL SUPPLIES
_ paper towels
_ toilet paper
_ furniture polish
_ glass cleaner
_ laundry detergent
_ spot remover
_ matches
_ butane lighter
_ charcoal lighter fluid
_ charcoal
_ first aid kit
_ fire extinguisher

17

EQUIPMENT

The romantic Italian dinner I planned for the first night of our trip to Niagara Falls would have made Julia Child green with envy. Regretfully, I did not get to prepare my marvelous dinner. I forgot to bring my skillet as well as the corkscrew.

Although the evening was depressing, it was not a major tragedy. My disappointment made me resolve not to repeat my folly in the future. A simple checklist of essential equipment would have easily compensated for my forgetfulness.

I suggest you scan my equipment list then make your own list, adding or eliminating items based on what is important in your food preparation. When you are satisfied it is complete, make photocopies. Use your individualized list to check off each item as you load your camper. The photocopied list will prove a valued friend, eliminating unhappy and unnecessary surprises.

Avoid unpleasant discoveries by making certain that the baking pans/dishes used in your oven and microwave and the storage containers used in your refrigerator actually fit in them. My RV oven, microwave, and refrigerator are considerably smaller than the ones I have in my kitchen.

For long trips I take almost all of the items on my list. Obviously, for short trips and "weekenders" many items are not necessary.

EQUIPMENT LIST

COOKING
Coffee pot
12-inch skillet and lid
10-inch skillet and lid
1 or 1½ qt. saucepan
   and lid
2 or 2½ qt. saucepan
   and lid
Double boiler and lid
4 or 6-qt. stew pot
   and lid
Broiler pan
Espresso coffee pot
Portable grill

MIXING/MEASURING
3 mixing bowls (small,
   medium, & large)
Set of measuring spoons
1 c. liquid measuring cup
2 c. liquid measuring cup
Set of dry measuring cups
Sifter
Jigger

MECHANICAL FRIENDS
Drip coffee maker
Toaster
Food processor
Blender
Microwave oven
Mixer and beaters

BAKING
15x10x1-inch rimmed
   baking sheet
13x9-inch glass baking
   dish
11x7-inch glass baking
   dish
9-inch square glass
   baking dish
9x5x3-inch metal loaf
   pan
8½x4½x2½-inch glass
   loaf pan
10-inch ceramic pie
   pan
9-inch springform pan
2 9-inch cake pans
8-inch cake pan
Cake rack
9-inch metal pie pan
9-inch glass pie pan
8-inch metal pie pan
14-inch pizza pan
1-qt. ceramic baking
   dish and lid
8½-inch round glass
   mixing bowl with
   cover for microwave
2-3 pot holders
Oven mitt

EATING UTENSILS
Knives, forks, soup
    spoons, & teaspoons
China (plates, cups,
    saucers, & salad
    bowls)
Serving bowls
Platter
Glasses
2-3 small bowls (for
    sauces/condiments)
2-3 medium bowls (for
    sauces/condiments)
Parfait glasses
Clear glass coffee mugs
Fondue forks

FOOD STORAGE
Small and medium
    refrigerator-to
    microwave plastic
    storage containers
    and lids
Pint and quart freezer
    containers and lids
    for dry storage
Small glass or plastic
    containers
Orange juice container
1 gallon plastic container
    for water (empty milk
    container)
Water container for
    refrigerator
Salad dressing cruet(s)

UTENSILS
2 spatulas
Wooden mixing spoons
Slotted spoon
2 small sharp knives
Large sharp knife
Large serrated knife
Cookie/biscuit cutter
Rolling pin (drinking
    glass with straight
    sides can substitute)
Can-opener
Corkscrew
Vegetable peeler
Grater
4-6 skewers
Kitchen scissors
Potato masher
Wooden mallet
Whisk
Meat thermometer
Oven thermometer
Refrigerator thermometer
Small strainer
Colander
Tongs (for grilling)
Swiss knife
Cutting board

MISCELLANEOUS
Cookbooks/recipes
Dish pan
Dish cloth
Dish towels
Extension cords
Thermos
Mini-vacuum
Whisk broom
Iron
Linens

EXTRA TOUCHES...
Napkin rings
Placemats
Cloth napkins
Trays (for dining
  outside in chair
  when there's no
  table)
Flower vase
Candles
Candle holders

LOADING YOUR CAMPER/RV

After the maiden voyage with our RV, my husband and I laughingly decided to name it "The Triple R," short for rearrange and rearrange and rearrange. We learned the importance of organization the hard way--by experience. Do not consider the placement of your supplies as trivial; a well thought out system will save considerable time and frustration.

PLACEMENT OF SUPPLIES

Place frequently used items in convenient locations, such as cabinets and drawers. Seldom used items are best stored in storage crates/boxes in less accessible areas.

It also makes good sense to stock your shelves with frequently used items in the front. Likewise, pack your crates/boxes with items placed in them according to when you plan to use them. In other words, the beans for next week can go in first, on the bottom.

When stocking shelves, boxes, etc., put all like items in one area if possible. For example, all of my baking supplies occupy one shelf. I use two crates to store infrequently used canned goods--canned meat and fish occupy one crate while vegetables, soups, and sauces are located in another. Loading your camper in this manner will eliminate endless searching and sorting.

LABELS

If an item is not stored in its original container, a label is highly recommended. Your memory may not be as reliable as you may think!

STORAGE CONTAINERS

Modular refrigerator-to-microwave containers are well suited to RV storage. They use space efficiently because they are stackable.

I also like pint and quart freezer containers for dry foods such as flour, sugar, rice, etc. Stackable containers are preferred.

Small bottles and jars are versatile storage containers. Mustard, pimiento, olive, maraschino cherry, and caper glass containers are great for small quantities of a variety of ingredients. The small bottles enable me to have a well-stocked mini-liqueur cabinet as well as an elaborate selection of condiments in my refrigerator.

Plastic medicine bottles make excellent spice containers. They are available in a variety of sizes and can be inexpensively purchased at the drugstore. Their versatility enables me to keep fifty spices on hand. I store them in a rectangular baking pan placed in a drawer; labels are taped on the bottle cap. I recommend that you do not use child-resistant caps.

I use two Tupperware containers with lids to store my refrigerated fruits and vegetables. A 14x6x5-inch rectangular container stores vegetables and an 11½x5 3/4x 3½-inch container holds fruits. Their airtight lids insure freshness and also make them suitable for use in an ice chest or cooler.

SAFETY TIPS

Your camper/RV refrigerator may not be as reliable as the one you have in your home. Many RV refrigerators can only reduce the temperature 40°- 60° below the outside temperature. Keep a refrigerator thermometer in the refrigerator and check it occasionally. That way you can be certain that your food is sufficiently chilled to avoid spoilage.

Resist the temptation to cook while your camper is under way. Regardless of whether you are using a crockpot or an enclosed oven, an unexpected stop or sharp turn could send the pot and/or its contents flying or cause the door to open. The gas flames make you vulnerable, too. If you are involved in an accident or drive by an accident in which propane or gas is leaking, the consequences could prove disastrous.

APPETIZERS

MUSHROOM-ALMOND PATÉ

1/2 lb. mushrooms, rinsed and dried (do not substitute canned mushrooms)
2 T. margarine
1/2 c. chopped onion
1 garlic clove, chopped
1/2 c. slivered almonds
1/2 t. salt
1/8 t. coarse black pepper
2 t. soy sauce
2 t. Worcestershire sauce
8-oz. pkg. cream cheese
4 slices bacon, cooked and crumbled
Garnish: fresh chopped parsley, crisp bacon curl
Serve with: crackers

Slice mushrooms. Melt margarine in skillet; add mushrooms, onion, and garlic. Sauté until most of liquid has evaporated. Remove from heat.

Finely grind almonds in food processor. Add all ingredients, including mushroom mixture. Process until smooth. Refrigerate for 1 hour or until well chilled, then mold into ball. Roll in parsley, then garnish top of paté with bacon curl. Serve with crackers.
Serves 4.

QUICK PATÉ

4 oz. braunschweiger liver sausage
1/4 c. butter
4 oz. cream cheese
1 small garlic clove, quartered
1 t. Worcestershire sauce
1 t. soy sauce
1/4 t. coarse black pepper
1/8 t. garlic powder
1/8 t. onion salt
1 T. chopped green onion (green part only)
1 t. parsley
Serve with: sliced French bread, unpeeled apple
  wedges, sour pickles

Place all ingredients in food processor; process
until smooth. Serve immediately or store covered in
refrigerator until serving time. Use as a spread
for French bread or apple wedges. Accompany with sour
pickles. Serves 4.
VARIATION: place mixture in mold lined with plastic
wrap. Chill until firm. Unmold and serve.

REFRIED BEAN DIP

1-lb. can refried beans
1 lb. process cheese spread, shredded (I recommend
  Velveeta)
Garnish: tortilla chips, cherry tomato, fresh parsley
  sprig
Serve with: tortilla chips

Place beans and cheese in saucepan or in microwave dish. Heat on stove or in microwave until melted, stirring frequently. Spread into serving dish. Garnish rim of dish with tortilla chips. Place cherry tomato and parsley in center for color. Serve with tortilla chips. Serves 6-8.

CHILE CON QUESO

1 T. margarine
1/2 c. chopped onion
1/2 c. chopped green pepper
1/2 c. chopped canned tomatoes, well drained
2 eggs
1 T. chopped canned green chilies, or to taste
1 lb. process cheese spread, shredded (I recommend Velveeta)
Serve with: tortilla chips

Melt margarine in large skillet. Add onion and green pepper. Sauté until soft; do not brown. Remove from heat then stir in tomato and eggs. Mixture will look curdled. Add chilies and cheese. Return to stove. Cook on low heat, stirring constantly, until cheese is completely melted and mixture is smooth. Continue to cook until mixture thickens to the consistency of pudding, about 5 minutes. Pour into serving dish. Serve with tortilla chips. Serves 6-8.

DILL DIP

8-oz. pkg. cream cheese, softened
1 c. sour cream
2 T. finely chopped green onion (use green part only)
2 t. parsley
2 T. dill, heaping
1 T. Worcestershire sauce
1/2 t. beau monde seasoning
1/2-3/4 t. garlic salt
Green food coloring, optional
Serve with: crisp raw vegetables

Combine all ingredients. Refrigerate for at least 30 minutes before serving. Serve with raw vegetables. Serves 4-6.

TARAMOSALATA

2-oz. jar red roe (reserve 1/2 t. for garnish)
1 T. reconstituted lemon juice
1 c. mayonnaise
1 T. chopped onion
1/2 medium garlic clove, chopped
large slice wheat bread, torn into pieces
Garnish: reserved roe
Serve with: French bread, cut into cubes

Combine all ingredients in blender until smooth. Transfer mixture to bowl. Cover and chill at least 12 hours or overnight.

To serve: spread mixture into serving dish. Garnish center with reserved roe. Gig French bread cubes with toothpicks and use as dippers. Serves 4-6.

LIPTAUER CHEESE SPREAD

8-oz. pkg. cream cheese, softened
1/2 c. margarine or butter, softened
1 T. caraway seeds, pulverized in blender
1 T. paprika
1 T. chives
1 T. finely chopped green onion, heaping
3 anchovy fillets, drained and finely chopped
2 t. capers, drained
1 T. Dijon mustard
Serve with: pumpernickel bread, crackers

Place all ingredients in medium mixing bowl. Using electric mixer, combine until completely smooth. Spoon into serving bowl. Excellent spread on pumpernickel bread or crackers. Serves 4.
VARIATION: chill mixture until firm enough to handle. Roll into ball. Cover tightly and refrigerate until firm, about 4-5 hours. Let stand at room temperature for 1 hour before serving.

ITALIAN CHEESEBALL

2 8-oz. pkgs. cream cheese
2 medium garlic cloves, finely chopped
1 c. grated Parmesan cheese
Serve with: crackers

Cut cream cheese into cubes; place in microwave dish. Drop in garlic. Heat on high in microwave for 1-2 minutes or until cheese is softened. Stir in Parmesan. Chill until firm enough to handle, then shape into ball. Let stand at room temperature for 30 minutes before serving. Serve with crackers. Serves 6-8.

PIMIENTO CHEESEBALL

4-oz. jar chopped pimiento, well drained
8 oz. sharp Cheddar cheese, shredded
1/4 c. salad dressing
Garnish: dark green lettuce leaf
Serve with: crackers

Drain pimiento thoroughly between two paper towels. Place pimiento, cheese, and salad dressing in a medium mixing bowl. Using hand, combine. Form mixture into ball. Serve immediately, or cover and store in refrigerator until time to serve. Present cheeseball on dark green lettuce leaf. Serve with crackers. Serves 4.

MEXICAN CHEESEBALL

8 oz. sharp Cheddar cheese, shredded
2-oz. jar chopped pimiento, well drained
2 T. chopped canned green chilies, drained
2-3 T. salad dressing (use only enough to moisten)
1/4 t. sugar
1/4 t. garlic powder
1/2 t. dried minced onion
1/4 c. finely chopped onion
Garnish: chili powder, parsley
Serve with: crackers

Place all ingredients in medium mixing bowl. Using hand, combine. Form into ball. Roll in combination of chili powder and parsley. Serve immediately, or cover and store in refrigerator until time to serve. Serve with crackers. Serves 4.

SALSA

1-lb. can tomatoes, drained and chopped
1/3 c. tomato sauce
2 T. chopped canned green chilies
1/2 c. chopped onion
1 t. chili powder
1 T. vinegar, scant
1 medium garlic clove, chopped
Serve with: tortilla chips

Combine all ingredients. Cover and refrigerate for at least 2 hours to blend flavors. Serve with tortilla chips. Serves 4-6.

This is a delicious accompaniment for grilled chicken, steak, or fish, also.

BAGNA CAUDA

3 anchovy fillets
1 T. cold water
1/4 c. butter
1 small garlic clove, chopped
Serve with: crisp raw vegetables

Soak anchovies in water for 5 minutes. Drain off water, then rinse. Chop anchovies. Place chopped anchovy, butter, and garlic in microwave dish; cover with plastic wrap; heat on high until butter melts. Stir, then serve. Or, put ingredients in small saucepan and heat on stove. Use as dip for raw vegetables. Serves 2-4.

This is a delicious accompaniment for baked or broiled fish, also.

GREEN PEPPER SPREAD

1/2 c. chopped green pepper
1/2 c. apple jelly
2 t. sugar
1 t. cornstarch
2-3 drops green food coloring
Serve with: cream cheese, crackers

In small saucepan, bring pepper, jelly, and sugar
to boil. Boil uncovered for 5 minutes. Remove
from heat; pour into blender; blend until smooth.
Return mixture to saucepan. Remove 2 T. of liquid
and mix with cornstarch; pour back into saucepan;
add food coloring; stir until well combined. Heat
on low-to-medium heat, stirring constantly until
slightly thickened. Chill thoroughly before serving.
To serve: spread cream cheese on cracker then top
with pepper spread. Serves 2-4.
This is also delicious served hot as a sauce for
pork or lamb. Prepare and serve immediately or reheat
after refrigeration. Yields 1/2 cup sauce.
VARIATION: substitute red pepper for green pepper and
red food coloring for green. Delete sugar.

BLUE CHEESE DIP

8-oz. pkg. cream cheese, softened
1/2 c. sour cream
2 oz. blue cheese, crumbled
Serve with: crisp raw vegetables

Using electric mixer, combine all ingredients until
smooth. Refrigerate covered at least 1 hour before
serving. Use as dip for raw vegetables. Serves 2-4.
This is a good salad dressing, also.

SHRIMP LOG

4½-oz. can shrimp, rinsed and well drained (reserve
  5 shrimp for garnish)
1 c. cottage cheese, drained
2 t. grated Parmesan cheese
2 t. blue cheese, finely crumbled
1/16-1/8 t. lemon and pepper seasoning salt
1 T. chives
Garnish: 5 reserved shrimp
Serve with: crackers

Chop shrimp in blender or mash with fork. Place in small bowl; add other ingredients. Using spoon, mix thoroughly. Form into log. Garnish with reserved shrimp down center of log. Cover, then refrigerate at least 5 hours to blend flavors. Serve with crackers. Serves 4.

"SMOKED" SALMON SPREAD

7½-oz. can salmon, drained and boned
4 oz. cream cheese, cut into cubes
1/2 t. paprika
1/4 t. liquid smoke
1/4 t. Worcestershire sauce
1 t. caper juice
2 t. capers
1 T. lemon juice
1/8 t. coarse black pepper
1/4 c. chopped green onion
1/4 t. salt
Serve with: crackers

Place all ingredients in food processor; process until smooth. Place in bowl, then cover and refrigerate until well chilled. Serve with crackers. Serves 4.

ARIZONA CHEESE CRISP

Flour tortilla(s)
Shredded cheese (sharp Cheddar, Monterey Jack, or
  other favorite cheese)
Chopped canned green chilies, drained
Chopped red pepper or chopped pimiento
Chopped green pepper
Jalapeño pepper, if desired

Preheat oven to 375°. Place tortilla(s) on ungreased baking sheet. Sprinkle cheese over tortilla(s). Top with desired amount and combination of peppers. Bake until cheese melts. Cool 3-5 minutes. Place tortilla(s) on individual serving plate(s). Cut into wedges, then serve.

NIPPY CHEESE CANAPÉS

1½ c. shredded sharp Cheddar cheese
1½ t. Worcestershire sauce
1 T. chives
3 T. salad dressing
Small rye bread slices (I prefer Pepperidge Farm
  Party Rye Slices)

Place cheese, Worcestershire sauce, chives, and salad dressing in bowl. Using hand, combine. Spread mixture on bread. Place on ungreased baking sheet; broil until cheese melts and bread is lightly toasted. Serves 4.

QUESADILLAS

7-inch flour tortillas
Tomato paste
Chili powder
Chopped canned green chilies, drained
Sharp Cheddar cheese or Monterey Jack cheese,
shredded (use combination, if desired)
Garnish: cherry tomatoes, fresh parsley sprigs

Spread 2-3 t. tomato paste on a tortilla. Sprinkle with desired amount of chili powder and green chilies. Top with shredded cheese. Press a plain tortilla over mixture, like a sandwich. Place on ungreased baking sheet. Prepare more quesadillas and place on baking sheet. Bake in 400° oven for 5-10 minutes. Cool 5 minutes, then place each quesadilla on an individual serving plate. Cut into wedges. Garnish center of tortilla with cherry tomato and fresh parsley.

PARMESAN POPCORN

1/3 c. popcorn, unpopped
2 T. butter or margarine, melted
2 T. grated Parmesan cheese
Salt to taste

Pop corn in air popper, microwave, or on stove. Place popcorn in large mixing bowl or stew pot. Pour melted butter over popcorn and toss; add cheese and salt, then toss again. Serves 2-4.

SPICED PECANS

2 c. pecan halves
1 T. butter, melted
2 t. Worcestershire sauce
1/4 t. salt
1/8 t. coarse black pepper

Preheat oven to 300°. Place pecans in rimmed baking sheet. Toss with butter; add remaining ingredients and toss. Bake for 20 minutes. Drain on paper towel, then serve. Yields 2 cups.

CHEESY SMOKED WALNUTS

1 t. butter
1 c. walnut halves
1/4 t. hickory smoked salt
1/4 t. salt
1/8 t. coarse black pepper
2 T. grated Parmesan cheese

Melt butter in skillet. Add nuts and toss to coat. Heat until nuts are hot. Add remaining ingredients and toss to coat. Drain and cool on paper towel, then serve. Yields 1 cup.
CHEESY SMOKED PEANUTS: substitute 1 c. dry roasted unsalted peanuts for the walnuts.

MEXICAN STYLE DEVILED EGGS

4 hard-boiled eggs, shelled
3 T. salad dressing
1/4 t. salt, scant
1/2 t. cumin
1/2 t. chili pepper

Halve eggs lengthwise. Place yolk in bowl. Using fork to mix, add other ingredients (except egg whites), mashing to blend. Use mixture to fill egg whites. Serve immediately or cover and chill overnight. Serves 2.

WURST BITES

8-oz. pkg. refrigerated quick crescent dinner rolls
Mustard (Dijon, yellow or other)
4 hot dogs or wursts, cooked and cooled
Serve with: mustard (Dijon, yellow, or other)

Make a rectangle out of 2 rolls, sealing holes by pressing dough with fingers. Spread mustard on dough. Place hot dog on long edge of dough and roll up tightly; press to seal. Slice 1/2-inch thick. Place on greased baking sheet. Bake at 350° for 10 minutes. Serves 4-6.

CANTONESE EGG ROLLS

Filling:
1/2 lb. ground pork, cooked and drained
1 boiled chicken breast, finely chopped
4½-oz. can shrimp, drained, rinsed, and chopped
1 3/4 c. finely chopped fresh mushrooms (do not
   substitute canned mushrooms)
1¼ c. finely chopped celery
1¼ c. finely chopped green onion
1 egg
2 t. sugar
3/4-1 t. salt
1 T. soy sauce

Purchased egg roll skins
Vegetable oil
Serve with: Super-Quick Sweet and Sour Sauce (see
   page 89), Peanut Sauce (see page 126), and/or Dijon
   mustard

Combine all filling ingredients. Place a small
amount of filling on egg roll skin. Fold skin over
filling then turn in sides; roll up; wet edges to seal.
Deep-fry in hot oil for 3-5 minutes or until golden
brown. Serve with sauces. Yields 10 egg rolls.

Leftover egg rolls can be reheated. Place on
ungreased baking sheet. Bake in 400° oven for 10
minutes, turning after 5 minutes.

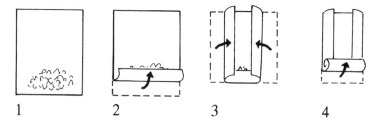

1   2   3   4

BEVERAGES

STRAWBERRY DAIQUIRIS

10-oz. pkg. sliced frozen strawberries in sugar, unthawed
2 T. milk
4½ jiggers white rum
5 ice cubes
Garnish: fresh strawberries

Cut frozen strawberry block into 6-8 pieces. Place all ingredients in blender; blend until slushy. It will be necessary to stop and stir. Pour into parfait glasses; garnish with strawberry. Serves 3-4.

BANANA DAIQUIRIS

2 bananas, sliced
3½ jiggers white rum
4 T. reconstituted lime juice
2 T. sugar
10 ice cubes

Place bananas, rum, lime juice, and sugar in blender; blend until smooth. Add ice and blend until slushy. Pour into parfait glasses. Serves 3-4.

VELVET HAMMER FRAPPÉ

1½ jigger apricot brandy
1 jigger Curaçao
1½ c. vanilla ice cream, firmly packed into liquid
  measuring cup

Place all ingredients in blender; blend until
smooth. Pour into parfait glasses. Serves 2.

SANTA FE FRAPPÉ

1 jigger Kahlúa
1 jigger dark rum
1 c. vanilla ice cream, firmly packed into liquid
  measuring cup
Garnish: chocolate sprinkles

Place all ingredients in blender; blend until
smooth. Pour into 2 parfait glasses. Garnish with
chocolate sprinkles. Serves 2.

GRASSHOPPER FRAPPÉ

1 jigger green crème de menthe
1½ jigger white crème de cacoa
1½ c. vanilla ice cream, firmly packed into liquid
  measuring cup
Garnish: whipped cream, fresh mint leaf

Place all ingredients in blender; blend until smooth.
Pour into parfait glasses. Garnish with whipped cream
and mint leaf. Serves 2.

SPIRITED CAFÉ MOCHA

1 jigger liqueur (Amaretto, Kahlúa, or hazelnut liqueur)
1 T. chocolate syrup
Hot coffee
Whipped cream
Sugar

Combine liqueur and syrup in coffee mug. Pour in hot coffee until two-thirds to three-fourths full. Top with whipped cream. Pass the sugar. Serves 1.

This is especially pretty served in clear glass mug.

MEXICAN HOT CHOCOLATE

2/3 c. milk
2 T. chocolate syrup
1 t. dry instant coffee
1/16 t. cinnamon

Combine milk and syrup. Heat in microwave or on stove until hot. Stir in coffee and cinnamon. Serves 1.

KAROL'S CINNAMON COFFEE

When preparing coffee in a percolator or by drip method, sprinkle a generous amount of cinnamon over the coffee grounds, then brew as usual. Preparing coffee in this manner imparts a wonderful cinnamon flavor to the coffee. This method is highly recommended when making coffee with the unpleasantly flavored water that is frequently encountered while camping.

My sister-in-law, Karol Ryan, contributed this delicious recipe.

ESPRESSO TOPPING FOR COFFEE

1 t. dry instant coffee, or to taste
1 t. water
4 oz. non-dairy whipped topping
Hot coffee
Sugar

Combine instant coffee with water. Add to whipped topping, stirring until smooth. Refrigerate until serving time. Pour hot coffee into mug. Add generous dollop of topping. Pass the sugar. Serves 4.

This is especially pretty served in clear glass mug.

GLUEHWEIN

4/5 qt. dry red wine
3-4 T. sugar
1 c. water
5 cloves
1 stick cinnamon
1/3 c. Curaçao liqueur

Combine, wine, sugar, water, cloves, and cinnamon in medium saucepan. Heat on high until very hot; do not boil. Reduce heat. Simmer uncovered for 15 minutes, stirring occasionally. Remove from heat; add Curaçao; stir, then pour into mugs. Spiciness increases as mixture cools. Serves 4.

This is especially pretty served in clear glass mug.

MULLED CRANBERRY-PORT

2 sticks cinnamon
6 whole cloves
4 c. cranberry juice
2 c. port

Place spices in medium saucepan. Pour in cranberry juice. Bring to boil uncovered. Reduce heat and simmer uncovered for 10 minutes. Add port. Heat until hot; do not boil. Remove spices and serve. Serves 6.

This is especially pretty served in clear glass mug.

BREADS

SWEET WHEATY BISCUITS

1 c. biscuit mix
1/3 c. wheat flour
2 T. light brown sugar, heaping
1/3 c. water, approximately

Preheat oven to 450°. Using a wooden spoon, mix together biscuit mix, flour, and sugar; mash out all sugar lumps. Add enough water to form a soft dough. Knead dough briefly on a floured surface. Roll out dough on floured surface to 8- or 9-inch circle, 1/3-inch thick. Cut biscuits with biscuit cutter or drinking glass. Dip cutter or glass into flour before cutting to avoid sticking. Place on ungreased baking sheet or in ungreased 8-inch cake pan. Bake in preheated oven for 10-12 minutes. Yields 8 biscuits.

CHEESE SCONES

1½ c. biscuit mix
1/2 c. sour cream or yogurt
1½ T. sugar
1/4 c. shredded sharp or mild Cheddar cheese, firmly
    packed
1/8 t. dry mustard
Garnish: dill or paprika

Preheat oven to 400°. Grease an 8-inch cake pan.
Place all ingredients in medium bowl. Mix quickly with
wooden spoon. Knead dough briefly on floured surface.
Divide dough into 8 parts; shape into balls, then place
in prepared pan. Garnish with a sprinkling of dill or
paprika. Bake in preheated oven for 15-20 minutes or
until lightly browned. Yields 8 scones.

RAISIN SCONES

1½ c. biscuit mix
1/2 c. sour cream or yogurt
2 T. sugar
1/4 c. raisins
1/4 t. cinnamon
Garnish: sugar, cinnamon

Preheat oven to 400°. Grease an 8-inch cake pan.
Place all ingredients in medium bowl. Mix quickly with
wooden spoon. Knead dough briefly on floured surface.
Divide dough into 8 parts; shape into balls, then place
in prepared pan. Garnish by sprinkling with sugar and
cinnamon. Bake in preheated oven for 15-20 minutes or
until lightly browned. Yields 8 scones.

SWEET "ROLLS"

Rolls:
1 c. biscuit mix
1/3 c. wheat flour
1/4 c. light brown sugar, lightly packed
1/4 t. cinnamon
1/4 c. raisins
1/4 c. chopped walnuts or pecans
1/4-1/3 c. water
Filling:
1 T. butter, cut into slivers
2 T. light brown sugar
Cinnamon
Topping:
1 T. butter
1 T. light brown sugar

Preheat oven to 425°. Place biscuit mix, wheat flour, light brown sugar, and cinnamon in medium bowl. Stir together using a wooden spoon; mash out all sugar lumps. Add raisins, nuts, and enough water to form a soft dough. Knead dough briefly on floured surface. Roll dough into an 8x11-inch rectangle on floured surface.

Top dough with 1 T. butter, cut into slivers. Sprinkle with 2 T. brown sugar and desired amount of cinnamon. Roll dough up from long side. Slice into 1-inch pieces using a serrated knife.

Prepare pan: melt 1 T. butter in 8-inch cake pan. Sprinkle 1 T. brown sugar in pan over butter. Gently place slices cut-side down in pan. Bake in preheated oven for 15-20 minutes or until lightly browned. Remove from oven and immediately flip pan onto serving platter. Scrape any remaining topping from pan and pat on rolls. Yields 8-10 rolls.

CHOCOLATE DATE-NUT BREAD

1½ c. boiling water
8-oz. pkg. chopped dates
1 c. chocolate chips
1/4 c. margarine
2½ c. sifted flour
1½ t. salt
1 t. baking powder
1 t. soda
1 egg
1 t. vanilla
1 c. sugar
1 c. chopped walnuts

Preheat oven to 350°. Grease and flour a
9x5x3-inch metal loaf pan.

Pour boiling water over dates in small bowl; set
aside to cool. Melt chocolate chips and margarine; set
aside to cool.

In large bowl, sift together flour, salt, baking
powder, and soda. Make well in dry ingredients and add
egg, vanilla, sugar, nuts, dates-water, and melted
chocolate-margarine. Stir with wooden spoon until
blended. Spoon batter into pan. Bake in preheated oven
for 1 hour-1 hour 10 minutes or until toothpick inserted
in center comes out clean. Cool completely before
serving. Prepare a day in advance of serving for mellowed
flavor.

CHOCOLATE RAISIN ZUCCHINI BREAD

2 eggs, well-beaten
1/2 c. + 1 T. vegetable oil
1 c. grated zucchini
1 c. sugar
1 t. vanilla
1¼ c. flour
1/4 t. baking powder
1/4 c. cocoa
1/2 t. salt
1/2 t. soda
1 t. cinnamon
1/2 raisins
1/2 c. chopped pecans or walnuts

Preheat oven to 350°. Grease and flour an 8½x4½x2½-inch glass loaf pan.
Combine eggs, oil, zucchini, sugar, and vanilla. Sift together flour, baking powder, cocoa, salt, soda, and cinnamon. Add dry ingredients to egg mixture. Stir in raisins and nuts. Pour batter into pan. Bake in preheated oven for 1 hour. Cool for 10 minutes, then remove from pan.

CHIPPETY-CHOCOLATE BREAD

1/2 c. margarine
1 c. sugar
1 egg
1 t. vanilla
2 c. sifted flour
1/3 c. cocoa
1 t. soda
3/4 t. salt
3/4 c. + 2 T. milk
2 t. vinegar
1 c. chocolate chips, divided

Preheat oven to 350°. Grease and flour an 8½x4½x2½-inch glass loaf pan.

Using electric mixer, cream margarine and sugar in medium bowl. Add egg and vanilla. Sift together flour, cocoa, soda, and salt; set aside. Combine milk and vinegar; add to creamed mixture; add dry ingredients. Stir in 2/3 c. chocolate chips. Pour batter into prepared pan. Sprinkle remaining 1/3 c. chocolate chips over batter. Bake in preheated oven for 50-60 minutes. Cool in pan 15 minutes; use two spatulas to lift bread out of pan. Cut with sharp knife when completely cool.

WHOLESOME WHEAT BEER BREAD

1¼ c. wheat flour
1¼ c. flour
1/4 c. wheat germ
1/4 c. uncooked rolled oats
4 t. baking powder
1 t. salt
1/4 c. light brown sugar, firmly packed
12-oz. can beer
1/3 c. margarine, melted

Preheat oven to 375°. Grease and flour an 8½x4½x2½-inch glass loaf pan.

Using wooden spoon, stir together wheat flour, flour, wheat germ, rolled oats, baking powder, salt, and brown sugar. Pour in beer; mix until well combined. Spread batter into prepared pan; top will appear very irregular. Pour 3-4 T. of melted margarine over batter. Bake in preheated oven for 1 hour-1 hour 10 minutes. Drizzle remaining margarine over bread after removing from oven.

COFFEE KUCHEN

2½ c. biscuit mix
1/2 c. sugar
1/2 c. light brown sugar, firmly packed
1 t. cinnamon
1/2 c. milk
1 T. dry instant coffee
2 T. unsalted butter, melted
1/2 t. vanilla
1 egg
2½ T. firm unsalted butter
Garnish: 1/4 c. chopped walnuts or pecans, cinnamon

Preheat oven to 400°. Grease and flour a 9-inch square glass baking dish.

Combine biscuit mix, sugar, light brown sugar, and cinnamon in medium bowl. Remove 3/4 c. and place in small bowl; set aside. This will be used to make topping.

Combine milk and instant coffee, stirring until coffee is completely dissolved. Make well in dry ingredients and pour in coffee-milk, melted butter, vanilla, and egg. When thoroughly mixed, pour into prepared pan.

Using fork, cut 2½ T. butter into reserved topping mixture until crumbly. Sprinkle topping mixture over batter, then sprinkle with nuts and cinnamon. Bake in preheated oven for 20-25 minutes. Prepare a day in advance of serving for mellowed flavor. Serve at room temperature. Serves 6-8.

RUM-RAISIN COFFEECAKE

Cake:
1½ c. biscuit mix
1/2 c. wheat flour
1/3 c. light brown sugar, firmly packed
1½ t. cinnamon
1 egg
1/2 c. milk
1/4 c. dark rum
3/4 c. raisins
Topping:
1/2 c. biscuit mix
1/3 c. light brown sugar, firmly packed
1 t. cinnamon
2½ T. firm margarine
Garnish: 1/2 c. chopped walnuts or pecans, cinnamon

Preheat oven to 400°. Grease and flour a 9-inch square glass baking dish.

Prepare cake: mix together biscuit mix, wheat flour, light brown sugar, and cinnamon. Add egg, milk, rum, and raisins, stirring until well combined. Spread into prepared pan.

Prepare topping: combine biscuit mix, light brown sugar, and cinnamon. Using fork, cut margarine into dry ingredients until crumbly. Sprinkle topping over batter, then sprinkle with nuts and cinnamon. Bake in preheated oven for 15-20 minutes or until tester inserted in center comes out clean. Prepare a day in advance of serving for mellowed flavor. Serve at room temperature. Serves 6-8.

BOURBON-APPLE COFFEECAKE: prepare Rum-Raisin Coffeecake substituting 1/4 c. bourbon for dark rum and 1 c. pared chopped apple for 3/4 c. raisins.

STRAWBERRY BREAKFAST CAKE

Cake:
2 c. biscuit mix
1 egg
3/4 c. strawberry preserves
1 t. vanilla
1/2 t. almond
1 t. imitation strawberry flavoring
1-2 T. milk
5 drops red food coloring
Topping:
1/3 c. light brown sugar, firmly packed
1/2 c. biscuit mix
2½ T. firm margarine
Glaze:
2 T. strawberry preserves
1 T. water
Garnish: 2 T. sliced almonds, confectioners' sugar

Preheat oven to 350°. Grease and flour a 9-inch square glass baking dish.

Prepare cake: using spoon, combine cake ingredients; spread into prepared pan. This is a thick batter.

Prepare topping: mix light brown sugar and biscuit mix. Using fork, cut margarine into dry ingredients until crumbly. Sprinkle topping and 2 T. sliced almonds over batter. Bake in preheated oven for 20-25 minutes.

Prepare glaze: combine preserves and water. Drizzle over cake while hot. Cool 15 minutes.

Garnish with a dusting of confectioners' sugar, then serve. Serves 6-8.

NOTE: the surface of this cake is very irregular.

DELUXE APPLE PANCAKES

1 c. biscuit mix
1 T. sugar
1/2 t. cinnamon
1 t. vanilla
1/2 c. milk
1 egg
1 c. pared chopped apple
Vegetable oil

Place all ingredients except apples and oil in medium bowl. Using wooden spoon, quickly combine until ingredients are well moistened. Heat approximately 1 T. oil in pancake griddle or frying pan until hot. Pour about 1/4 c. batter into pan for each pancake. Sprinkle chopped apple on batter. Pancakes are ready to flip when the surface of the pancake starts to bubble. After flipping the pancake, lower the heat then continue cooking until done. Place pancakes on warm platter in single layer. Add more oil to pan and cook remaining batter. Yields 5-6 pancakes.

PECAN PANCAKES: prepare Deluxe Apple Pancakes but delete cinnamon. Substitute 1 c. chopped pecans for 1 c. chopped apple.

BLUEBERRY SYRUP

1/2 c. blueberry pie filling
1/4 c. maple or maple flavored syrup

Combine pie filling and syrup. Heat until bubbly. Yields 3/4 cup.

YORKSHIRE PUDDING

2 eggs
1 c. milk
1 c. sifted flour
1/2 t. salt
1/4 t. ground thyme
1 t. parsley
1 T. roast-beef drippings
1 T. margarine, melted
1/4 c. margarine

Preheat oven to 450°. Beat eggs with electric mixer. Add milk, flour, and seasonings; mix until combined. Scrap down sides, then beat 2 minutes; batter will be thin. Stir in meat drippings and 1 T. margarine, melted.

Put remaining margarine in 9-inch square glass baking dish; place in preheated oven. Heat until very hot, approximately 3-5 minutes.

Remove pan from oven; pour batter into hot pan; return to oven and bake for 10 minutes. Reduce heat to 375° and bake for 20 additional minutes or until crust is lightly browned and puffed. Cut into squares. Serve on platter with roast beef. Serves 6.

NOTE: traditional recipes for Yorkshire Pudding recommend serving it immediately after removing from the oven. Although it is prettier when served after baking, for convenience I prefer to prepare it in advance. Cut some fat off the roast and fry in order to get 1 T. drippings. Reheat the pudding uncovered in a 350° oven for 20-30 minutes. Do not reheat in the microwave. The pudding will lose its crispness.

NEW YORK DELI PIZZA

Dough:
1 t. dry yeast
3/4 c. warm water
1 t. sugar
3/4 t. salt
1 T. vegetable oil
1½ c. flour
1/2 c. wheat flour
Toppings:
1/3 c. tomato paste
1 large garlic clove, chopped
1 t. oregano
1 t. basil
Salt and coarse black pepper
Meat (select one or combine): 2 oz. sliced pepperoni;
    2-4 slices sandwich ham, chopped; 1 c. cooked and
    crumbled Italian Meatloaf (see page 109); 1 c.
    cooked and crumbled Italian Meatballs (see
    page 110), or 1 c. cooked and crumbled turkey
    sausage
6-oz. jar marinated artichokes, drained and chopped
10-12 black olives, halved
1 T. vegetable oil
4-6 oz. mozzarella cheese, sliced
Grated Parmesan cheese

Preheat oven to 425°. Mix yeast with warm water,
stirring until dissolved. Add sugar, salt, and oil to
yeast mixture.

Place flours in medium bowl; stir. Pour in yeast
mixture. Using a wooden spoon, stir until mixture
forms a ball, approximately 20 strokes. Cover bowl
with damp towel or plastic wrap then set in warm
place for 5 minutes.

Grease a 14-inch pizza pan. Grease hands; spread dough on pizza pan by patting with fingers. Bake in preheated oven for 5-7 minutes or until crust is set; do not brown. Remove from oven.

Increase oven heat to 450°. Spread tomato paste over dough. Sprinkle chopped garlic, seasonings, meat, chopped artichoke, and olives over crust; drizzle with oil. Bake in preheated oven for 15-20 minutes or until crust is lightly browned. Remove from oven and add cheeses; return to oven and bake until cheese melts, approximately 5 minutes. Serves 2-3.

STROMBOLI

Pizza dough (see page 56)
3-4 T. tomato paste
1 large garlic clove, chopped
1 t. basil
Coarse black pepper
1 t. Italian seasoning
4 slices sandwich ham, each slice cut in half
1 T. Dijon mustard, heaping
4-6 oz. mozzarella cheese, sliced
Grated Parmesan cheese

Preheat oven to 425°. Mix dough as for New York Deli Pizza, but let rise in warm place until dough doubles in size, approximately 1 hr. Punch down dough; let dough rest for 5 minutes.

On well-floured wax paper, roll dough into 14-inch circle. Spread with tomato paste. Sprinkle with chopped garlic, and seasonings. Top half of dough with ham slices. Spread ham slices with mustard. Place sliced cheese on ham then sprinkle with Parmesan cheese.

Moisten edge of dough with water then fold tomato paste side of dough over ham side; seal tightly by pressing and crimping together. Use additional water to seal, if necessary. Grease a baking sheet. Turn sheet upside down and place over filled dough. Flip sheet and dough; carefully peel dough off wax paper if it sticks. Bake for 25-30 min. or until browned. Let stand 5 minutes before slicing. Serves 2-3.

PISSALADIÈRE

8-oz. can refrigerated quick crescent dinner rolls
1 c. chopped onion
1 T. margarine
2-3 T. tomato paste
20-24 pitted black olives, halved
1 large garlic clove, chopped
1 t. oregano
1 t. basil
Salt and coarse black pepper
1 T. vegetable oil

Preheat oven to 375°. Separate dough into 8 triangles. Press into ungreased 14-inch pizza pan, leaving a 2-inch border. Bake 5-7 minutes or until dough is set.

Meanwhile sauté onion in margarine. Remove partially baked dough from oven; spread tomato paste over dough. Sprinkle onions over dough, then add olive halves; sprinkle chopped garlic and seasonings over dough; drizzle with oil. Bake at 375° for 10-15 minutes or until crust is golden brown. Serves 2-4.

MAIN DISHES

SPAGHETTI ALLA CARBONARA

1/2 lb. bacon, chopped
4 eggs
3 T. grated Parmesan cheese
1/4 t. salt
Coarse black pepper to taste
2 T. butter or margarine
2 servings spaghetti or linguine, cooked al dente
  and drained (approximately 2 c.)
Serve with: grated Parmesan cheese

Fry bacon in large skillet until brown and crisp.
Drain bacon pieces on paper towel. Wipe out pan and set
aside. In small bowl combine eggs, cheese, salt, and
pepper. Melt butter in skillet. Add spaghetti, bacon
pieces, and egg mixture all at once. Stir, then continue
to cook on medium until mixture reaches desired
consistency. Pass additional Parmesan cheese. Serves 2.

SPAGHETTI ALL'AMATRICIANA

1/2 lb. bacon, chopped
1 c. chopped onion
1/2 c. chopped red pepper
1/2 c. dry white wine
2-3 T. butter (do not substitute margarine)
1 T. grated Parmesan cheese, heaping
14½-oz. can tomatoes, chopped and drained
1 T. tomato paste
1/4 t. coarse black pepper
Additional butter and grated Parmesan cheese, optional
Serve with: 2 servings spaghetti or linguine, cooked
    al dente and drained (approximately 2 c.), grated
    Parmesan cheese

Fry bacon in large skillet until brown and crisp.
Drain bacon pieces on paper towel. Add onion and red
pepper to bacon grease in pan. Sauté gently until limp,
but do not brown. Drain off grease from pan. Add bacon
pieces, wine, butter, cheese, tomatoes, and tomato paste
to pan with onion and red pepper. Simmer uncovered for
10-15 minutes or until sauce gets thick and rich.
Season with pepper and additional butter and Parmesan
cheese, if desired. Pour sauce over hot spaghetti.
Pass the Parmesan cheese. Serves 2.

ROULADEN

1½ lb. thinly sliced round steak
Salt and coarse black pepper
Dijon mustard
Catsup
Uncooked bacon slices, cut in half
Chopped onion
Vegetable oil
Sauce:
10¼-oz. can beef gravy
1 medium onion, chopped
2 T. brown sugar
3 T. vinegar
2 t. Worcestershire sauce
1 bay leaf, crumbled
1/4 t. ginger
1/4 t. salt
Coarse black pepper to taste
1-2 T. cornstarch, optional

Place beef slices between 2 pieces of wax paper;
pound both sides with wooden mallet. Season one side of
each slice with salt and pepper. Spread seasoned side of
each slice with mustard then catsup; top with one-half
bacon slice; sprinkle with chopped onion; roll up each
slice and secure with toothpick.

Heat oil in large skillet; add rouladen and brown on
all sides; do not drain. In bowl, combine all sauce
ingredients (except cornstarch); pour sauce into pan with
meat. Bring to boil, then lower heat to simmer. Cover
and simmer for 1 hour. Remove meat to warm platter.

Use cornstarch to thicken sauce, if necessary. Mix
1/4 c. sauce with cornstarch, then return to pan. Stir,
then heat on medium until thickened. Pour some sauce
over meat; pass remaining sauce. Serves 4.

ROAST BEEF WITH ENCHILADA SAUCE

4 lb. sirloin tip roast
Salt and coarse black pepper
Enchilada Sauce:
1/2 c. chopped onion
Vegetable oil
1-lb. can tomatoes, chopped and drained, then pureed
  in blender
1 t. chopped garlic (approximately 4 medium cloves)
2 t. chili powder
1/2 t. oregano
1½ t. cumin
1/4 t. coarse black pepper
2 8-oz. cans tomato sauce
2 t. lemon juice
Garnish: fresh parsley

Preheat oven to 325°. Line a shallow rimmed baking pan with aluminum foil.

Remove excess fat from roast. Pat roast dry, do not wash; season with salt and pepper. Place roast in pan. Insert meat thermometer in thickest part of meat, being careful not to have tip of thermometer against fat. Time required to cook roast varies considerably due to size and shape variations; however, allow approximately 15-20 minutes per pound for rare (140°), 22-25 minutes per pound for medium (160°), and 27-30 minutes per pound for well done (170°). When roast reaches desired doneness, remove from oven and let stand 15 minutes before carving.

Prepare Enchilada Sauce: in medium saucepan, sauté onion in small amount of vegetable oil. Add remaining sauce ingredients; simmer uncovered for 10 minutes.

Slice beef and place on platter. Pour sauce down center of slices. Pass additional sauce. Serves 6.

MARINATED ROAST BEEF

2-3 lb. sirloin tip roast
Salt and coarse black pepper
Marinade:
1 c. water
1 c. Pink Chablis
10 peppercorns
1 bay leaf
1 garlic clove, chopped
4 whole cloves
1 t. dried rosemary, crushed
1/4 t. thyme leaf
1/2 t. ground marjoram

4 strips bacon

Season roast with salt and pepper. Place in large glass bowl (do not marinate in metal or porous ceramic bowl).

Mix marinade ingredients and pour over roast in bowl. Cover and marinate in refrigerator for 24 hours, turning meat occasionally.

Remove roast from marinade; discard marinade. Wrap bacon around roast and secure with toothpicks.

Preheat oven to 325°. Line a shallow rimmed baking pan with aluminum foil. Bake as directed in Roast Beef with Enchilada Sauce (see page 63). When roast reaches desired doneness remove from oven and let stand 15 minutes before carving. Remove toothpicks. Serves 3-4.
VARIATION: a venison roast may be substituted for beef.

CAJUN ROAST BEEF

4 lb. sirloin tip roast
1 t. paprika
1 t. salt
1 t. coarse black pepper
1½ t. oregano
1 t. thyme leaf
1/8 t. cayenne pepper, or to taste
1 t. garlic powder
1 t. onion powder

Preheat oven to 325°. Line a shallow rimmed baking pan with aluminum foil. Pat roast dry, do not wash. Mix seasonings and rub on roast. Insert meat thermometer then roast according to directions in Roast Beef with Enchilada Sauce (see page 63). When roast reaches desired doneness remove from oven and let stand 15 minutes before carving. Serves 6.

CREOLE MUSTARD STEAK

Sirloin or flank steak
Salt and coarse black pepper
Creole mustard or spicy brown mustard

Season steak with salt and pepper; spread mustard on both sides. Grill until reaches desired doneness.

GRILLADES

Creole Sauce:
1/3 c. butter
2/3-3/4 c. chopped green pepper
1 c. chopped onion
2 medium garlic cloves, chopped
1 t. marjoram leaf
1/8 t. coarse black pepper
1/2 t. salt
1-lb. can tomatoes, chopped and undrained

2 lb. sirloin steak
Salt and coarse black pepper
3 T. butter
2 medium garlic cloves, chopped

Prepare sauce: melt 1/3 c. butter in medium skillet; add green pepper, onion, and garlic. Sauté until translucent; do not brown. Stir in seasonings and tomatoes. Simmer 15 minutes uncovered over medium heat. Keep warm while cooking meat.

Cut steak into 4 servings; season with salt and pepper. Melt 3 T. butter in large skillet then add garlic and steak. Sear steak on high heat. Reduce heat to medium. Continue to cook until steak reaches desired doneness. Remove to serving platter; pour some sauce over meat. Pass remaining sauce. Serves 4.

TERIYAKI STEAK

1/2 c. dry sherry
1/4 c. soy sauce
1/4 c. brown sugar
1½ lb. sirloin steak

Combine sherry, soy sauce, and brown sugar, stirring until sugar is dissolved. Set aside.

Remove excess fat from steak, then cut into 1½-inch wide strips. Place steak in shallow glass dish; pour marinade into dish. Toss to coat meat, then let stand for 15 minutes at room temperature. Drain meat, reserving marinade. Grill over hot coals. Heat reserved marinade and serve with steak. Serves 2.

STEAK WAIKIKI

1 lb. sirloin steak, 1/2-inch thick
Marinade:
1/2 c. orange juice
3 T. soy sauce

Mix orange juice and soy sauce, then set aside. Put steak in plastic bag, then pour marinade into bag. Seal. Place in shallow glass dish. Marinate overnight in refrigerator, turning occasionally. Drain steak, discarding marinade. Grill until reaches desired doneness. Serves 2.

SHISH KABOB

2 lb. sirloin steak, cut into 1-inch cubes
Salt and coarse black pepper
Marinade:
1/2 c. vegetable oil
1/4 c. soy sauce
1/2 c. red wine
2 large garlic cloves, chopped
2 T. catsup
Coarse black pepper to taste

2-3 medium green peppers, cut into 1½-inch squares
2-3 medium onions, quartered
Serve with: rice

Season steak cubes with salt and pepper, then place in shallow glass dish. Set aside. Combine marinade ingredients and pour over steak; toss to coat. Cover tightly and refrigerate overnight.

Assemble kabobs: drain meat, reserving marinade. On a skewer, thread a vegetable and a meat cube, alternating. Baste with marinade while grilling. Discard marinade after grilling. This is excellent served with rice. Serves 4.

CARNE ASADA

1½ lb. sirloin steak, cut into 1½-inch strips
Marinade:
2/3 c. tomato juice
1 T. vegetable oil
1/4 t. coarse black pepper
1/2 t. oregano
3/4 t. cumin
1 t. chili powder
2 t. vinegar
2 t. lemon juice
1 medium garlic clove, chopped
Serve with: flour tortillas, salsa, sour cream,
   guacamole, reserved marinade

Combine marinade ingredients. Put steak in
plastic bag; pour marinade into bag and seal; place
bag in shallow glass dish. Refrigerate 8 hours or
overnight, turning bag occasionally. Drain marinade
and reserve. Grill meat until reaches desired doneness.

To serve: place steak strips on tortilla, then
add desired toppings (salsa, sour cream, and guacamole).
Roll up to eat. Dip in reserved marinade, if desired.
Serves 2-3.

BISTECCA ALLA PIZZAIOLA

1/4 c. vegetable oil
1 lb. sirloin steak (1/2-inch thick), cut into 2 servings
3 medium garlic cloves, chopped
1-lb. can tomatoes, chopped and drained
1/2 t. oregano
1/2 t. basil
1/4 t. coarse black pepper
1/4 t. salt
1/2 c. white wine
3 T. butter (do not substitute margarine)

Heat oil in skillet until very hot. Add steak and
garlic to pan. Using high heat, sear steak on both sides.
Remove pan from heat; add tomatoes, spices, and wine.
Return to stove and cook on medium until steak is
almost done (approximately 5 minutes for medium rare).
Remove steak to warm platter, then finish sauce.

Add butter to sauce in pan. Turn heat to high. Continue
cooking uncovered until sauce is rich and thick. Pour sauce
over steak. Serves 2.

ZESTY STEAK SALAD

2 c. cooked and cubed sirloin steak (preferably grilled)
15- or 16-oz. can kidney beans, drained
1/2 c. chopped celery
1/2 c. chopped onion
2 T. chopped sweet pickle or chopped dill pickle
1/4 c. salad dressing
1 T. chili sauce
Salt and coarse black pepper to taste
Garnish: lettuce leaves

Combine all ingredients in medium bowl. Season with salt and pepper. Serve in lettuce lined bowl or on individual serving plates lined with a lettuce leaf. Serves 2-3.

BEEF AND PEPPERS

1 lb. sirloin steak, cut into 1/2-inch strips
2 T. soy sauce, divided
Coarse black pepper
Vegetable oil
2 large green peppers, cored and cut into strips
1 large garlic clove, chopped
2 t. cornstarch, divided
1 T. beef bouillon
2 T. water
Serve with: hot rice

Place beef strips in shallow glass dish. Toss with 1 T. soy sauce and black pepper. Marinate at room temperature while continuing recipe.

Heat oil in large skillet. Sauté green pepper strips and garlic until pepper is very limp. Remove from pan and drain on paper towel. Add additional oil to pan and heat until very hot. Meanwhile toss beef with 1½ t. cornstarch. Add beef strips to hot pan; sauté until beef loses its pink color. Pour off excess oil. Combine beef bouillon, water, 1/2 t. cornstarch, and 1 T. soy sauce then pour into pan. Return green pepper to pan. Stir, then cook on medium until sauce is slightly thickened. Serve over hot rice. Serves 2.

ZIPPY BBQ STEAK

1 c. orange juice
3/4 c. catsup
1/4 t. garlic powder
1/2 t. dried minced onion
3 T. soy sauce
2 t. yellow mustard
1 large garlic clove, chopped
2 lb. sirloin steak
Salt and coarse black pepper

Combine orange juice, catsup, garlic powder, onion, soy sauce, mustard, and garlic in saucepan. Simmer 5 minutes uncovered. Cool to room temperature.

Season steak with salt and pepper. Place in shallow glass dish then pour cooled marinade over steak; toss to coat. Marinate for 20 minutes at room temperature. Drain steak, reserving marinade. Grill (or broil) steak until reaches desired doneness. Do not baste steak while grilling. Heat remaining marinade and serve as sauce. Serves 4-5.

HERB MARINATED STEAK

1 c. Italian dressing
1 large garlic clove, chopped
1/2 t. parsley
1/4 t. oregano
1/4 t. basil
1½ lb. sirloin steak
Salt and coarse black pepper

Combine dressing, garlic, and spices. Set aside. Season steak with salt and pepper. Place in shallow glass dish; pour marinade over steak; toss to coat. Cover dish and refrigerate 8 hours or overnight. Drain off marinade and discard. Grill steak until reaches desired doneness. Serves 2-3.

BEEF STROGANOFF

1½ lb. sirloin steak, cut into 3/4-inch cubes
Butter or margarine
1 medium onion, chopped
3 garlic cloves, chopped
2 T. flour
1/2 t. salt
1/4 t. coarse black pepper
4-oz. can sliced mushrooms, drained
10 3/4-oz. can cream of chicken soup
1/2-3/4 c. sour cream
Serve with: egg noodles

In large skillet, sauté beef in butter until no longer pink. Remove beef from pan to warm plate. Pour off meat juices from pan. Melt additional butter in pan, then stir in onion and garlic. Sauté until onion is translucent; do not brown. Add flour and mix. Stir in seasonings, mushrooms, and soup; simmer uncovered 5 minutes. Drain meat cubes and return to pan; simmer 5 minutes. Gradually stir in sour cream, heating thoroughly. This is excellent served over egg noodles. Serves 3-4.

MANICOTTI

1 egg
3/4 c. cottage cheese
1/3 c. grated Parmesan cheese
1/3 c. cubed mozzarella cheese
1 t. parsley
1/8 t. salt
Dash of coarse black pepper
4 5-inch manicotti shells, cooked al dente and drained
Ragù sauce
Garnish: shredded mozzarella cheese

Preheat oven to 350°. Grease an 11x7-inch glass baking dish. In small bowl combine egg, cottage cheese, Parmesan cheese, mozzarella cheese, parsley, salt, and pepper. Use mixture to stuff manicotti shells.

Pour enough ragù sauce in baking dish to cover bottom. Lay stuffed manicotti in pan. Pour ragù sauce over manicotti to cover. Bake uncovered in preheated oven for 30-35 minutes or until thoroughly heated. Serves 2.

CHICKEN PIQUANT

6 smoked sausage links (I prefer Oscar Meyer)
Vegetable oil
4 chicken breasts, skinned
Salt and coarse black pepper
2 8-oz. cans tomato sauce
14½-oz. can tomatoes, chopped and undrained
1/4 t. coarse black pepper

In large skillet, brown sausage in vegetable oil. Drain on paper towel. When cool, slice into bite-size pieces.

Season chicken with salt and pepper. Fry chicken in sausage drippings until brown on both sides. Add remaining ingredients; bring to boil, then reduce heat. Cover and simmer for 30 minutes, turning chicken after 15 minutes. Serves 4.

CHICKEN WITH CHUTNEY SAUCE

4 chicken breasts, skinned
Salt, coarse black pepper, and paprika
Vegetable oil
1 c. chopped onion
1-lb. can whole berry cranberry sauce
1/3 c. orange juice
1/2 t. ginger, scant
1/4 t. sage
1/4 t. coarse black pepper
1 t. paprika
1/4 t. salt
1/4 t. garlic powder
Serve with: wild rice

Season chicken with salt, pepper, and paprika. Heat oil in skillet. Brown chicken on both sides. Add onions and sauté until translucent.

Combine cranberry sauce with remaining ingredients in small saucepan; heat until mixture boils. Pour over chicken in skillet. Simmer uncovered for 30 minutes. If sauce gets too thick add more orange juice. This is excellent served with wild rice. Serves 4.

CHICKEN PAPRIKA

1 T. vegetable oil
1 c. chopped onion
1/2 c. chopped red pepper
1/2 c. chopped green pepper
4 chicken breasts, skinned
Salt and coarse black pepper
1/2 c. chicken bouillon
1/4 t. salt
1 T. paprika
1/4 t. coarse black pepper
1/4 t. ground marjoram
14½-oz. can tomatoes, chopped and well drained
1/2 c. sour cream
1-2 T. flour, optional
Serve with: egg noodles

Heat oil in large skillet. Add onion and peppers; sauté until softened. Drain vegetables on paper towel. Season chicken with salt and pepper then add to pan. Using high heat, brown on both sides.

Combine bouillon with seasonings. Pour into skillet with chicken. Stir in chopped tomato and drained vegetables. Bring to boil, then reduce heat. Cover and simmer for 25-30 minutes, turning chicken after 15 minutes; stir occasionally. Remove cooked chicken pieces to heated platter.

Combine sour cream with sauce. If sauce is thin, thicken with flour: mix 1/4 c. sauce with flour, then return to pan. Heat until thick and hot. Pour sauce over chicken. Serve with egg noodles. Serves 4.

CHICKEN-POT PIE

Filling:
2 c. cooked chicken, skinned and cubed
10 3/4-oz. can cream of mushroom soup
10-oz. pkg. frozen mixed vegetables, cooked and
  drained
1 T. Worcestershire sauce
1/4 t. coarse black pepper
Salt to taste
1/3 c. milk
8 slices cooked bacon, drained and crumbled
Pastry:
1½ c. biscuit mix
2 T. margarine
1 egg
1 t. parsley
1-3 T. water

Preheat oven to 375°. Grease a 9-inch metal pie pan.
Combine all filling ingredients, except bacon pieces.
Spread filling into pie pan; sprinkle with bacon pieces.

Prepare pastry: using fork, combine biscuit mix and
margarine until mixture resembles coarse crumbs. Using
wooden spoon, stir in egg, parsley, and enough water to
make a soft dough. Roll dough into circle on a floured
surface.

Place pastry on top of filling, pressing edge of dough
firmly to pan rim. Crimp edges to seal. Using fork, cut
steam vents. Decorate surface with pastry cutouts. If
desired, cover edge of crust with strip of aluminum foil
to prevent excessive browning. Bake in preheated oven for
25-35 minutes or until filling is hot and crust is lightly
browned. Serves 4.

DOUBLE-BAR RANCH BBQ CHICKEN

4-6 chicken breasts, skinned
Marinade:
1/2 c. vegetable oil
1 c. cider vinegar
2 T. salt
1½ t. poultry seasoning
1 large garlic clove, chopped
1/4 t. coarse black pepper
1/4 c. sugar
3 T. catsup

Place chicken in glass bowl. Combine marinade ingredients and pour over chicken. Cover tightly, then marinate in refrigerator for 5 hours. Drain chicken, discarding marinade. Grill chicken until done. Serves 4-6.

CHILI CHICKEN

4 chicken breasts, skinned
Salt and coarse black pepper
3 c. chili (homemade or 2 15-oz. cans chili)
1 c. shredded sharp Cheddar cheese

Preheat oven to 375°. Grease a 13x9-inch glass baking dish. Season chicken with salt and pepper, then lay in pan with meaty side up. Pour chili over chicken, coating well. Cover with foil and bake in preheated oven for 30 minutes. Remove foil and bake an additional 30 minutes. Remove chicken from oven and sprinkle with cheese. Return to oven and bake until cheese melts. Serves 4.

ITALIAN STYLE ROAST CHICKEN

4 chicken breasts, skinned
Salt and coarse black pepper
Thyme leaf
2 medium garlic cloves, finely chopped

Preheat oven to 375°. Grease a 13x9-inch glass baking dish. Season chicken with salt, pepper, and thyme. Lay chicken in pan with meaty side up. Sprinkle garlic over chicken. Bake uncovered in preheated oven for 1 hour. Serves 4.

CHICKEN MARENGO

4-6 chicken breasts, skinned
Salt and coarse black pepper
2 garlic cloves, chopped
1-lb. can tomatoes, chopped and undrained
6-oz. can tomato paste
2 4-oz. cans sliced mushrooms, drained
1 bay leaf
1/2 t. thyme leaf
3/4 t. salt
1/4 c. white wine
Garnish: pitted black olives

Preheat oven to 375°. Grease a 13x9-inch glass baking dish. Season chicken with salt and pepper. Lay chicken in pan with meaty side up. Combine garlic, tomatoes, tomato paste, mushrooms, seasonings, and wine; pour over chicken. Bake uncovered in preheated oven for 55 minutes. Remove from oven; sprinkle black olives into pan. Bake 5 minutes to heat olives. Serves 4-6.

CHICKEN CACCIATORA

4-6 chicken breasts, skinned
Salt and coarse black pepper
2 garlic cloves, chopped
1-lb. can tomatoes, chopped and undrained
6-oz. can tomato paste
2 medium onions, cut into 8 equal sections
1 T. parsley
1 bay leaf, crumbled
1/2 t. salt

Preheat oven to 375°. Grease a 13x9-inch glass baking dish. Season chicken with salt and pepper, then lay in dish with meaty side up. Combine remaining ingredients in small bowl; pour over chicken. Bake uncovered in preheated oven for 1 hour. Serves 4-6.

POLLO AL FORNO

6 chicken breasts, skinned
Coarse black pepper
1/2 c. flour
1 t. salt
1/2 c. grated Parmesan cheese
1/4 c. sesame seeds
2 t. parsley

Preheat oven to 375°. Grease a 13x9-inch glass baking dish. Season chicken with pepper. Combine flour, salt, cheese, sesame seeds, and parsley. Coat chicken with flour mixture. Place chicken in dish with meaty side up. Bake uncovered in preheated oven for 1 hour. Serves 4-6.

COQ AU VIN

4 slices bacon
1 c. chopped onion
1 large garlic clove, chopped
4 chicken breasts, skinned
Salt and coarse black pepper
4-oz. can sliced mushrooms, drained
3 T. butter (do not substitute margarine)
1 bay leaf
1/2 t. tarragon
1 t. parsley
1/4 t. coarse black pepper
1 c. white wine
1 c. chicken bouillon
1 T. flour, optional
Serve with: hot rice

Sauté bacon in large skillet, then drain on paper towel.
Crumble when cool. Add onion and garlic to bacon
drippings in skillet; sauté. Drain on paper towel. Do
not drain fat from pan.

Season chicken with salt and pepper. Brown chicken in
bacon drippings, 5 minutes each side. Add all ingredients
(except flour) to pan; bring to boil. Reduce heat; cover
and simmer for 25-30 minutes.

If sauce is thin, thicken with flour. Mix 1/4 c. sauce
with flour, then return to pan. Stir, then heat until
thickened. This is particularly good served with rice.
Serves 4.

BIRD OF PARADISE CHICKEN SALAD

2 medium chicken breasts, boiled and skinned
1/2 medium apple, peeled and chopped
1/4 c. chopped onion
3 T. sour cream
3 T. mayonnaise
1 t. curry
Salt to taste

Cube chicken. Combine chicken pieces with apple and onion. Set aside.

Combine sour cream, mayonnaise and curry; toss with chicken mixture. Season with salt. Chill for least 1 hour to blend flavors. Serves 2.

CALIFORNIA STYLE CHICKEN SALAD

2 medium chicken breasts, boiled and skinned
2 T. salad dressing
2 T. sour cream
1 T. Dijon mustard
3 hard-boiled eggs, chopped
1/4 c. chopped onion
1/2 c. chopped black olives
1 T. tarragon, scant
Salt and coarse black pepper

Cube chicken; set aside. Combine salad dressing, sour cream, and mustard. Add chicken and remaining ingredients, mixing thoroughly; adjust seasonings. Chill at least 30 minutes to blend flavors. Serves 2.

SOUTHERN FRIED CHICKEN

Chicken pieces, washed (do not remove skin)
Salt and coarse black pepper
Flour
Shortening (I recommend Crisco)

Wash, but do not dry chicken. Season with salt and pepper. Place flour in small paper bag. Add chicken one or two pieces at a time; shake to coat.

Heat approximately 1½-inches of shortening in a large skillet until very hot. Chicken must sizzle when placed in pan. Brown pieces on both sides for approximately 5 minutes total time. Watch carefully so as not to brown too darkly. Reduce heat to low and fry for 30 minutes, turning after 15 minutes. Drain on paper towel, then serve.

My Mother contributed this delicious recipe.

NORTHERN FRIED CHICKEN

Chicken pieces, skinned
Salt and coarse black pepper
Allspice
Flour
Vegetable oil

Wash, then dry chicken. Season with salt, pepper, and allspice. Coat with flour. Heat oil until hot. Add chicken pieces and brown on both sides. Reduce heat to low, then cover and cook for 30 minutes, turning after 15 minutes.

My Mother-in-law contributed this delicious recipe.

CHICKEN-PEPPER KABOBS

3 chicken breasts, skinned and deboned
Salt and coarse black pepper
Sauce:
3 T. catsup
2 t. steak sauce (I recommend A-1)
1 t. Worcestershire sauce
1/4 t. liquid smoke

10 2-inch red pepper squares
10 2-inch green pepper squares

Cut deboned chicken into bite-size pieces. Season with salt and pepper. Set aside.

Prepare sauce: mix catsup, steak sauce, Worcestershire sauce, and liquid smoke. Set aside.

Assemble chicken and peppers on four skewers: thread with one red pepper square, two pieces chicken, then one green pepper square, two pieces chicken, etc., ending with pepper. Baste with sauce.

Grill until done, turning once. Baste with sauce while grilling. Serves 2-3.

BAKED CHICKEN PECAN

4 chicken breasts, skinned
Salt and coarse black pepper
1 c. crushed pecans (I crush in blender)
2 T. sesame seed
1 t. paprika

Preheat oven to 375°. Grease a 13x9-inch glass baking dish. Season chicken with salt and pepper. Combine crushed pecans, sesame seed, and paprika; coat chicken with nut mixture. Place chicken in dish with meaty side up. Bake in preheated oven for 1 hour. If chicken pieces brown too quickly cover pan with aluminum foil. Serves 4.

STIR-FRIED CHICKEN AND BROCCOLI

3 chicken breasts, skinned and deboned
1 T. vegetable oil
3 T. soy sauce, divided
3 T. sherry, divided
1/2 c. chopped onion
2 c. fresh broccoli flowerets, steamed (or 10-oz. pkg. frozen chopped broccoli, thawed and drained)
8-oz. can water chestnuts, drained and sliced
1-2 t. cornstarch, optional

Cut deboned chicken into bite-size pieces. Heat oil in skillet until hot. Add chicken and 2 T. soy sauce and 2 T. sherry; stir-fry until meat loses its pink color. Add onion; stir-fry until onion is translucent. Add broccoli, water chestnuts, and remaining 1 T. soy sauce and 1 T. sherry; stir-fry until all ingredients are well heated.

If sauce is thin, thicken by sprinkling cornstarch over mixture. Stir, then cook over low heat until sauce thickens. Serves 2-3.

BAKED "BLACKENED" CHICKEN

1 t. paprika
1 t. salt
1 t. coarse black pepper
1½ t. oregano
1 t. thyme leaf
1/8 t. red cayenne pepper, or to taste
1 t. garlic powder
1 t. onion powder
4-6 chicken breasts, skinned
Melted butter

Preheat oven to 375°. Grease a 13x9-inch glass baking dish. Combine seasonings. Dip chicken in butter, then sprinkle with seasoning mixture. Place chicken in dish with meaty side up. Bake uncovered in preheated oven for 1 hour. Serves 4-6.

CHICKEN FRIED RICE

Vegetable oil
1/2 c. chopped green pepper
3/4 c. chopped celery
1 c. chopped onion
2 boiled chicken breasts, skinned and cubed
3 T. soy sauce, divided
3 T. sherry, divided
1 c. cooked and chilled rice, unseasoned
2 eggs
2 T. milk or water

Heat oil in large skillet until hot. Stir-fry green pepper, celery, and onion until vegetables are limp; do not brown. Add chicken, 2 T. soy sauce and 2 T. sherry; simmer 1 minute. Stir in chilled rice.

In small mixing bowl, combine eggs with milk. Push all ingredients in skillet to one side then pour in egg mixture. Using medium heat, cook as for scrambled eggs. When eggs reach desired doneness mix with other ingredients in pan. Stir in remaining 1 T. soy sauce and 1 T. sherry. Adjust seasonings then serve. Serves 2-3.

CHICKEN CURRY

2 T. margarine
1 apple, peeled and finely chopped
1 c. chopped onion
2 t. curry, divided
10 3/4-oz. can cream of mushroom soup
1/2 c. milk
1/2 c. sour cream
1/8 t. salt
4 boiled chicken breasts, skinned and cubed
Serve with: hot rice

Melt margarine in large skillet. Add apple, onion, and 1 t. curry then sauté; do not brown. Stir in soup, milk, sour cream, salt, remaining 1 t. curry, and chicken cubes. Heat thoroughly. Serve over rice. Serves 4.

CHICKEN GUMBO WITH SMOKED SAUSAGE

4 slices bacon
2 chicken breasts, skinned
4 smoked sausage links, sliced 1/4-inch thick (I prefer
  Oscar Meyer)
1½ c. chopped onion
1 c. chopped green onion
1 c. chopped green pepper
2-3 T. bacon drippings
1/4 c. flour
1 qt. water
2 chicken bouillon cubes
1/4 t. salt
1/2 t. coarse black pepper
Serve over: hot rice

In large skillet, fry bacon until crisp. Drain bacon,
then crumble when cool. Remove 2-3 T. bacon drippings
from pan and reserve. Brown chicken and sausage in
remaining bacon drippings; drain chicken and sausage.
Add onion, green onion, and pepper to pan. Sauté until
onion is translucent; drain vegetables. Wipe out pan.

Prepare roux: add reserved 2-3 T.bacon drippings
to skillet, then stir in flour. Cook over low-to-medium
heat, stirring constantly until well blended. Continue
to cook until roux is the color of a copper penny,
approximately 5-10 minutes.

Put roux in stew pot. Add drained vegetables, bacon,
chicken, sausage, 1 qt. water, bouillon cubes, salt, and
pepper to stew pot. Bring to boil, then reduce heat; cover
and simmer for 1 hour, stirring occasionally. Remove pan
from heat. Remove chicken from gumbo; let gumbo and
chicken cool separately for 15 minutes. Cube chicken

then return to gumbo. Serve over hot rice in soup bowl. Serves 4.

The gumbo is better if prepared a day in advance of serving. Store covered in refrigerator overnight. Skim off excess fat, then heat thoroughly.

STIR-FRIED CHICKEN WITH LETTUCE

4 chicken breasts, skinned and deboned
1 egg
2 T. cornstarch
2 T. soy sauce
1 t. sugar
Vegetable oil
Super-Quick Sweet and Sour Sauce:
1/2 c. strawberry preserves
2 t. vinegar
Garnish: shredded lettuce
Serve with: hot rice

Cut deboned chicken into bite-size cubes. Set aside.

Combine egg, cornstarch, soy sauce, and sugar in small bowl. Pour into an 11x7-inch glass dish. Add chicken pieces, stirring to coat; marinate 10 minutes at room temperature.

Heat vegetable oil in large skillet until hot. Add chicken pieces and stir-fry until done. Drain.

Prepare sauce: combine preserves and vinegar. Heat until hot.

To serve: place shredded lettuce around rim of serving platter or bowl. Fill with hot chicken pieces. Serve with Super-Quick Sweet and Sour Sauce and hot rice. Serves 4.

PASTA WITH WHITE CLAM SAUCE

2 T. olive oil
3 T. butter, divided (do not substitute margarine)
1 t. chopped garlic
1/3 c. chopped green onion
2 6½-oz. cans minced clams, drained with juice
   reserved
1/2 c. clam juice
1 t. parsley
1/4 t. coarse black pepper
2 servings spaghetti or linguine, cooked al dente
   and drained (approximately 2 c.)
Serve with: grated Parmesan cheese, French
   bread

Heat oil and 2 T. butter in skillet, then add garlic
and onion; sauté briefly. Add clam juice; simmer
5 minutes. Stir in clams and parsley. Heat until sauce
is thickened. Place hot pasta in serving bowl; toss
pasta with remaining 1 T. butter and 1/4 t. pepper.
Pour sauce over pasta. Serve with grated Parmesan
cheese. Use French bread to "sop up" sauce in true
Italian fashion. Serves 2.

ITALIAN BAKED CORNISH HEN

2 20-oz. each Cornish hens
Salt and coarse black pepper
1 T. vegetable oil
Garnish: fresh parsley
Serve with: lemon wedges

Preheat oven to 400°. Line a shallow rimmed baking sheet with aluminum foil; grease. Cut hens lengthwise along entire backbone. Split open to lay flat, cracking the bone. Wash and dry thoroughly. Season hens with salt and pepper, then place on sheet with meaty side up. Sprinkle 1 T. oil over hens. Bake uncovered in preheated oven for 30 minutes. Reduce heat to 350° and bake 30-35 minutes. If necessary, tent with aluminum foil to prevent excessive browning. Cut skin at leg to test for doneness; hen is done when juices run clear and the meat is white.

Remove to serving platter. Garnish platter with lemon wedges and fresh parsley. Serves 2.

SOUTH-OF-FRANCE CORNISH HEN

2 1-lb. each Cornish hens
Salt and coarse black pepper
Thyme leaf
Ground marjoram
2 large garlic cloves, chopped

Preheat oven to 400°. Line a shallow rimmed baking sheet with aluminum foil; grease.

Generously season inside of hens with salt and pepper. Season outside of hens with salt, pepper, thyme, and marjoram. Place hens with meaty side up on prepared baking sheet. Sprinkle 1 chopped garlic clove over each hen.

Bake uncovered in preheated oven for 30 minutes. Reduce heat to 350° and bake for 30 minutes. If necessary, tent with aluminum foil to prevent excessive browning. Cut skin at leg to test for doneness; hen is done when juices run clear and the meat is white. Serves 2.

MARYLAND CRAB CAKES

1 slice bread, torn into pieces
1 egg
2 t. Dijon mustard
1/4 t. salt
1/4 t. coarse black pepper
6-oz. can crabmeat, drained and cartilage removed
　　(or 6 oz. fresh crabmeat)
1 T. salad dressing
Vegetable oil

Combine bread, egg, mustard, salt, pepper, crabmeat, and salad dressing. Form into 4 patties. Fry in oil until lightly browned and firm, turning once. Serves 2.

ROAST DUCK WITH RAISIN-RASPBERRY SAUCE

4 lb. duckling
Salt and coarse black pepper
Raisin-Raspberry Sauce:
1/2 c. red raspberry preserves
1/3 c. water
1/4 c. raisins
1 T. Amaretto

Preheat oven to 350°. Line a shallow rimmed baking pan with aluminum foil; grease.
Wash duck, then season with salt and pepper. Score skin at 1-inch intervals for a crisp skin. Place duck, breast side up in prepared pan. Roast uncovered in preheated oven for 1 hour. Pour off fat. Reduce heat to 325° and continue to roast uncovered for 1 hour-

1 hour 15 minutes. Five minutes before done baste once with sauce (see below). Duck is done when leg feels soft when pressed, and the legs can be easily jiggled up and down. Baste once more before removing from oven. Let stand 15 minutes before carving. Pass remaining sauce. Serves 2-4.

Prepare sauce: in small saucepan heat preserves, water, and raisins until mixture boils. Turn off heat; stir in Amaretto.

EGG ENCHILADA

1½ c. salsa
1 Monterey Omelet, prepared in 12-inch skillet (see page 96)
10- or 12-inch flour tortilla
Garnish: 1/2 c. shredded Monterey Jack cheese, chopped green onion

Preheat oven to 375°. Grease an 11x7-inch glass baking dish. Pour enough salsa in pan to cover bottom. Set aside.

Prepare Monterey Omelet. Gently place unfolded omelet on tortilla. Roll up tortilla and omelet as for enchilada (see page 112); using 2 spatulas carefully transfer to casserole. Pour salsa over tortilla to cover. This will keep the tortilla moist and prevent toughness while baking.

Bake uncovered in preheated oven for 25 minutes. Remove from oven and top with cheese. Return to oven 5 minutes to melt cheese. Garnish with chopped green onion. Slice with sharp knife. Use spatula to serve. Serves 2-3.

PAIN PERDU

2 eggs
1/2 c. milk
1 t. vanilla
1/4 t. cinnamon
4-6 slices bread
Butter or margarine
Serve with: your favorite syrup

Beat eggs, milk, vanilla, and cinnamon with whisk or fork. Pour into shallow container. Dip bread slices in mixture, making sure to generously coat both sides. Fry in hot butter until browned on both sides. Serve with warmed syrup. Serves 2.

CHRISTMAS TOAST

2 eggs
2/3 c. eggnog
1/4 t. nutmeg
4-6 slices bread
Butter or margarine
Serve with: maple syrup

Beat eggs, eggnog, and nutmeg with whisk or fork. Pour into shallow container. Dip bread slices in mixture making sure to generously coat both sides. Fry in hot butter until browned on both sides. Serve with maple syrup. Serves 2.

UOVA 'MPRIATORIO (EGGS IN HELL)

Vegetable cooking spray
3/4-1 c. tomato juice
4 eggs
Salt and coarse black pepper

Spray a medium skillet with cooking spray. Pour in tomato juice then bring to boil. Drop in eggs. Season with salt and pepper. Cook until eggs reach desired doneness. Using spatula, transfer eggs to serving platter; pour sauce over eggs. Serves 2-4.

GREEN CHILI QUICHE

2 c. shredded Monterey Jack cheese
3 T. canned chopped green chilies, drained
1 c. biscuit mix
1 c. milk
4 eggs
1/4 t. coarse black pepper
1/2 t. salt

Preheat oven to 375°. Grease a 10-inch ceramic baking pan. Sprinkle cheese into pan, then top with chilies. Put remaining ingredients into blender; blend on high for approximately 15 seconds; pour mixture into pan. Bake for 15-20 minutes in preheated oven. Quiche is done when turns golden brown and knife inserted in center comes out clean. Let stand 5-10 minutes before serving. Serves 4.

BASIC OMELET

4 eggs
1/8 t. salt
2 T. cold water
Butter or margarine

Beat all ingredients together with whisk or fork until well mixed, but not frothy.

Melt butter in 12-inch omelet pan or skillet; heat until very hot. Pour in egg mixture all at once. Reduce heat to medium. Let mixture set, then lift mixture gently with fork or spatula, tilting pan to let uncooked egg run underneath. Continue to cook until fairly dry on top and light brown on bottom. If desired, put pan in broiler to cook top until firm.

Serve the omelet open or fold in half with spatula. Serves 2.

EASY CHEESE OMELET: when omelet reaches desired doneness, place 4-5 slices American process cheese on top. Broil until melted. Fold in half, then serve.

WESTERN: sauté 1/4 c. chopped onion and 1/4 c. chopped green pepper in 1 T. butter or margarine. When vegetables change color add 1 T. more butter. Pour in egg mixture all at once. Cook as directed for basic omelet. Variation: add 1/3 c. chopped ham to egg mixture before pouring into pan.

HERB: add 1 T. parsley, 1/4 t. ground marjoram, and 1/2 t. tarragon to egg mixture. Cook as for basic omelet. When done spread with approximately 4 oz. softened cream cheese. Heat briefly in broiler, then fold in half and serve.

MONTEREY: prepare basic omelet. When omelet reaches desired doneness, top with 1 T. canned chopped

green chilies (or to taste) and 1 c. shredded Monterey
Jack cheese. Broil until cheese melts. Fold in half
then serve.

HUEVOS RANCHEROS

Egg
Flour tortilla
Salsa

Fry egg until reaches desired doneness. Meanwhile
heat tortilla in oven or in microwave until warm.
Heat salsa, too.
To assemble: place warm tortilla on serving plate.
Top with fried egg. Pour desired amount of salsa over
all.
VARIATION: serve egg on warmed rice, deleting tortilla.

SCRAMBLED EGGS WITH MUSHROOM

1/4 c. milk
1/4 c. undiluted cream of mushroom soup
4 eggs
Butter or margarine
Coarse black pepper

Combine milk and soup; stir in eggs. Heat butter
in skillet until hot; add egg mixture all at once,
cooking as for scrambled eggs. Season with pepper.
Serves 2-4.

CHEDDAR TART

2 c. shredded sharp Cheddar cheese
1 c. biscuit mix
1 c. milk
4 eggs
1/2 t. salt
Garnish: paprika

Preheat oven to 375°. Grease a 10-inch ceramic baking pan. Sprinkle cheese into pan. Put remaining ingredients in blender; blend on high for 15 seconds. Pour into pan. Bake for 15-20 minutes in preheated oven. Tart is done when knife inserted in center comes out clean. Garnish with paprika. Let stand 5-10 minutes before serving. Serves 4.
MUENSTER DILL TART: substitute Muenster cheese for Cheddar cheese and add 1 t. dill to ingredients in blender. Delete paprika.

CREOLE BUTTER SAUCE

1/4 c. butter, melted
1 T. Creole mustard or spicy brown mustard
Serve with: fish

Briskly whisk warm melted butter with mustard. Serve with fish. Yields 1/4 cup.

CRUSHED-CROUTON BREADED FISH

Croutons, any flavor
Salt and coarse black pepper
Fish fillets or steaks, rinsed and dried

Preheat oven to 350°. Grease a glass baking dish. Crush croutons in blender or food processor. Season fish with salt and pepper; coat with crushed croutons. Place fish in baking dish. Bake in preheated oven for 25-30 minutes. Fish is done when flakes with fork.

BAKED FISH, ITALIAN STYLE

1 lb. fish fillets, rinsed and dried
Coarse black pepper
Breading:
1/2 c. flour
1 t. salt
1/2 c. grated Parmesan cheese
1/4 c. sesame seeds
2 t. parsley

Preheat oven to 350°. Grease a 13x9-inch glass baking dish. Season fish with black pepper. Combine breading ingredients; coat fish. Place fish in baking dish. Bake in preheated oven for 25-30 minutes. Fish is done when flakes with fork. Serves 2.

HICKORY BBQ FISH

1 lb. red snapper or halibut fillets, rinsed and dried
Sauce:
1/2 c. catsup
3 T. brown sugar
1 t. liquid smoke
1 T. Worcestershire sauce
1 T. vinegar
1 t. dry mustard
1/4 t. coarse black pepper

Preheat oven to 350°. Grease a 13x9-inch glass baking dish. Combine ingredients for sauce. Place unseasoned fish in baking dish; pour sauce over fish; turn to coat, then marinate at room temperature for 10-15 minutes. Bake in preheated oven for 25-30 minutes. Fish is done when flakes with fork. Remove fish to platter, then serve. Discard marinade. Serves 2-4.

LEMON-DILL CATFISH

1 lb. catfish fillets, rinsed and dried
Salt and coarse black pepper
Lemon and pepper seasoning salt
Dill
2 slices wheat bread, processed into crumbs

Preheat oven to 350°. Grease a 13x9-inch glass baking dish. Season fish with salt, pepper, lemon and pepper seasoning salt, and dill; coat with bread crumbs. Place fish in baking dish. Bake in preheated oven for 25-30 minutes. Fish is done when flakes with fork. Serves 2-4.

MUSTARD BUTTER SAUCE

1/4 c. butter, melted
1 T. Dijon mustard
1 t. Worcestershire sauce
1 t. parsley
Serve with: fish

Briskly whisk butter with remaining ingredients.
Serve with fish. Yields 1/4 cup.

HERBED FISHWICHES

1 c. boiled and flaked halibut or red snapper, well
  drained (approximately 1/2-2/3 lb.)
1 T. chopped onion
2 T. chopped green onion
1/2 c. cubed Muenster cheese
1/4 t. salt
1/4 t. coarse black pepper
1/2 t. dill, heaping
1 t. chives, heaping
2-3 hamburger buns
Mayonnaise or salad dressing

While fish is still hot, mix with remaining ingredients
(except buns and mayonnaise). Split buns. Broil both
sides of bottom bun halves until warm. Spread cut side
of bottom bun halves with mayonnaise. Top with fish
mixture. Broil filled bottom bun halves and both sides
of top bun halves until thoroughly heated. Spread top bun
halves with mayonnaise, then press onto filled bun halves
as for sandwich. Serves 2-3.

ITALIAN-BREADED FRIED TROUT

Pan-dressed whole trout, rinsed and dried
Salt and coarse black pepper
Italian seasoning
White corn meal
Vegetable oil

Season fish with salt and pepper. On outside of fish, rub on desired amount of Italian seasoning; coat with white corn meal. Heat oil in skillet until hot; add fish. Reduce heat. Fry fish approximately 4-6 minutes on each side. Fish is done when flakes with fork.

SPANISH SAUCE

1/2 c. chopped onion
1 large garlic clove, chopped
Vegetable oil
14½-oz. can tomatoes, chopped and undrained
2 t. capers, drained
1 t. parsley
2 t. Dijon mustard
1/2 c. halved black olives, drained
1/4 t. coarse black pepper
Serve with: fish

Sauté onion and garlic in oil until limp, but not browned. Add remaining ingredients. Bring to boil, then reduce heat to simmer. Cover and simmer for 10 minutes or until sauce thickens. Serve with fish. Serves 2-4.

ALMOND CRUSTED FISH

1 lb. red snapper fillets, rinsed and dried
Salt and coarse black pepper
3/4-1 c. whole almonds, crushed in blender
Serve with: melted butter

Preheat oven to 350°. Grease a 13x9-inch glass baking dish. Season fish with salt and pepper; coat with crushed almonds. Place fish in baking dish. Bake in preheated oven for 25-30 minutes. Fish is done when flakes with fork. Serve with melted butter.

BROILED SALMON
WITH PARMESAN TOPPING

1 lb. salmon fillets or steaks, rinsed and dried
Salt and coarse black pepper
Topping:
1/4 c. sour cream
2 T. grated Parmesan cheese

Line a broiler pan with aluminum foil, then grease. Season fish with salt and pepper. Broil fish 4 inches from heat source until almost done (4-6 minutes each side). Prepare topping: combine sour cream and Parmesan cheese. Remove fish from broiler; spread mixture on fish then return to broiler; broil until bubbly. Serves 2.
VARIATION: substitute halibut for salmon.

EASY TARTAR SAUCE

1/2 c. salad dressing
1 T. kosher dill pickle juice
1 T. chopped kosher dill pickle
1 T. chopped onion
Serve with: fish

Combine all ingredients. Cover and chill 10-15 minutes to blend flavors. Serve with fish. Yields 1/2 cup.

BROILED SALMON
WITH CREAMY HERB SAUCE

2-4 salmon steaks or fillets
Salt and coarse black pepper
Creamy Herb Sauce:
8-oz. pkg. cream cheese, softened
3-4 T. milk
2 t. dill
2 T. chives
1/4-1/2 t. garlic salt
2 t. lemon juice

Line a broiler pan with aluminum foil, then grease. Season salmon with salt and pepper. Broil fish 4 inches from heat source until flakes with fork, approximately 5-7 minutes each side.

Prepare sauce: in small saucepan or in microwave dish, add milk to softened cream cheese. Heat until hot, stirring frequently until smooth. Remove from heat source. Add remaining ingredients, stirring to combine. Yields 1 cup. Serves 2-4.

"JUST FOR THE HALIBUT" BURGERS

Halibut fillets, cut to fit buns
Salt and coarse black pepper
Flour
Vegetable oil
Tartar Sauce
Hamburger buns
Lettuce
Sliced tomato

Rinse and dry fillets. Season fish with salt and pepper; coat with flour. Fry in hot oil until flakes with fork. Spread Tartar Sauce on bun; top with fish; add lettuce and tomato; Serve as sandwich.

DELUXE TARTAR SAUCE

1/4 c. salad dressing or mayonnaise
1/4 c. sour cream
1 t. dill
2 T. finely chopped onion
2 T. chopped kosher dill pickle
1 T. kosher dill pickle juice
1 t. yellow mustard
1 T. chopped green onion
Serve with: fish

Combine all ingredients. Cover and chill 10-15 minutes to blend flavors. Serve with fish. Yields 2/3 cup.

HAM WELLINGTON

Pie Crust:
1½ c. flour
1/4 t. salt
1/2 c. shortening
1/4 c. ice water
Filling:
1 T. butter
1/2 c. chopped onion
1 slice wheat bread, cubed
4-oz. can mushroom pieces, drained
1/8 t. salt
1/8 t. coarse black pepper
1/8 t. thyme leaf
1/8 t. celery seed
1 t. parsley
1 T. milk, optional

8-oz. oval shaped cooked ham slice

Preheat oven to 400°. Prepare pie crust: combine flour and salt. Cut in shortening with fork until mixture resembles coarse crumbs. Pour in water, then mix with fork until dough holds together. On lightly floured surface, roll out dough. Cover with damp towel.
Prepare filling: melt butter in skillet; sauté onion. Add bread cubes, mushrooms, and seasonings to pan, tossing to coat. If mixture seems dry add milk to moisten. Line a rimmed baking sheet with aluminum foil, then grease. Place ham slice on sheet. Spread filling mixture on top of ham. Top with pastry. Cut pastry a little larger than ham slice, then tuck pastry under ham. Press on cut pastry flowers for garnish, if

desired (there will be left over pastry). Bake in preheated oven for 20-25 minutes or until crust is done. Broil to brown top of pastry.

Remove from oven. Loosen ham from foil with spatula. Use 2 spatulas to transfer ham to serving platter. Serves 2.

HAM JAMBALAYA

2 c. chopped onion
2 large garlic cloves, chopped
1/4 c. chopped celery
1 c. chopped green pepper
1/4 c. margarine
1-lb. can tomatoes, chopped and drained with juice
  reserved
1/3 t. salt
1/4 t. coarse black pepper
1/4 t. thyme leaf
1/4 t. chili powder
1 bay leaf, crumbled
2 c. cooked and chilled rice, lightly seasoned with salt
1½ c. cubed cooked ham
1/2-2/3 c. tomato juice

In large skillet, sauté onion, garlic, celery, and green pepper in margarine. Add tomatoes and seasonings to vegetables. Simmer covered 10 minutes, stirring occasionally. Stir in rice, ham, and tomato juice, starting with lesser amount. Simmer covered for 5-7 minutes. Turn off heat. Let stand covered on stove burner for 5 minutes. Serves 4.

PASTA WITH HAM AND CHICKEN SAUCE

3 T. margarine or butter
3 T. flour
1/4 t. salt
1¼ c. milk
1/4 t. coarse black pepper
1 large garlic clove, chopped
1/4 c. grated Parmesan cheese
1 boiled chicken breast, skinned and cubed
5 slices sandwich ham, cut into 1/2-inch strips
1/8 t. thyme leaf
1/2 t. basil
4-oz. can sliced mushrooms, drained
Serve with: 2 servings spaghetti or linguine,
    cooked al dente and drained (approximately 2 c.)

Melt margarine in small saucepan. Stir in flour and salt then heat until bubbly. Remove pan from heat; gradually stir in milk. Return pan to heat and cook over medium heat until thick, stirring constantly.

Add remaining ingredients to prepared white sauce. Simmer uncovered for 5-7 minutes to blend flavors and to heat thoroughly. Pour sauce over hot pasta. Serves 2.

CHILI

1 lb. ground beef
1 large onion, chopped
2 large garlic cloves, chopped
3 8-oz. cans tomato sauce
1-lb. can tomatoes, chopped and undrained
1-lb. can kidney beans, undrained
3 T. canned chopped green chilies, or to taste

1 T. + 1 t. chili powder
1 T. + 1 t. cumin
1 t. salt
Serve with: chopped onion, shredded Cheddar cheese

In large skillet, sauté beef until no longer pink. Drain off fat. Add onion and garlic to skillet with beef. Sauté over low heat until onion is translucent.

Transfer mixture to large stew pot. Add remaining ingredients. Simmer covered for 30 minutes, stirring occasionally. Serve with chopped onion and shredded cheese. Serves 4.

ITALIAN MEATLOAF

1 lb. ground beef
1 egg
1/4 c. catsup
2 slices wheat bread, torn into small pieces
2 garlic cloves, chopped
1 t. salt
1 t. Italian seasoning, scant
Garnish: hard-boiled egg, sliced
Serve with: ragù sauce or Napolitano Tomato Sauce
    (see page 110)

Preheat oven to 375°. Combine ground beef with remaining ingredients. Pack mixture into an 8½x4½x2½-inch glass loaf pan. Bake in preheated oven for 1 hour. Remove from oven; drain grease from pan, then turn out loaf onto serving platter. Garnish with row of sliced egg down center of loaf. Serve with ragù sauce or Napolitano Tomato Sauce. Serves 4.

SPAGHETTI AND ITALIAN MEATBALLS

Italian Meatballs:
2 slices wheat bread
1 lb. ground beef
1 t. salt
1 T. parsley
1 T. grated Parmesan cheese
1 egg
2 medium garlic cloves, chopped
1/8 t. coarse black pepper
Vegetable oil
Napolitano Tomato Sauce:
1-lb. can tomatoes, chopped and drained
2 large garlic cloves, chopped
1/4 c. vegetable oil
1 t. sugar
1 t. basil
1 t. oregano
Coarse black pepper to taste
1/4 t. salt
8-oz. can tomato sauce
Serve with: 4 servings spaghetti, cooked al dente and drained (approximately 4 c.), grated Parmesan cheese

Prepare meatballs: place bread in small bowl, then add enough water to cover. Let stand 2 minutes. Remove slices and squeeze out water. In medium bowl, combine bread with remaining ingredients. Shape into 1-inch balls. Lightly grease a large skillet with oil. Fry meatballs in skillet over low-to-medium heat until done. Turn as necessary.

Prepare sauce while frying meatballs: combine all ingredients in medium saucepan. Bring to boil, then reduce heat. Simmer uncovered for 15 minutes or until oil separates from tomatoes and the sauce has thickened.

To serve: Place cooked spaghetti on plate. Top with meatballs. Pour sauce over all. Pass Parmesan cheese. Serves 4.

ITALIAN SUBMARINE SANDWICH

1 recipe Italian Meatballs (see page 110)
1 recipe Napolitano Tomato Sauce (see page 110)
Submarine rolls

Prepare meatballs and sauce. Heat rolls. Place meatballs on rolls; pour over sauce. Serves 4.

FRITTATA

2 c. cooked spaghetti, well chilled
2 eggs
1/4 c. ragù sauce
Meat (select one or combine): 1 c. cooked and crumbled Italian Meatballs (see page 110), 1 c. cooked and crumbled Italian Meatloaf (see page 109), or 1 c. cooked and crumbled turkey sausage
1/4-1/3 c. grated Parmesan cheese
Salt and coarse black pepper
1/2 c. shredded mozzarella cheese or sharp Cheddar cheese
Serve with: ragù sauce

Preheat oven to 375°. Combine spaghetti with remaining ingredients. Taste, then correct seasonings. Turn into greased 9-inch glass pie pan. Bake in preheated oven for 20-25 minutes. Cut into wedges to serve. Pass additional ragù sauce. Serves 4.

BEEF AND BEAN ENCHILADAS

1 lb. ground beef
3/4 c. chopped onion
2 medium garlic cloves, chopped
1½ t. cumin
1½ t. chili powder
1/4-1/2 t. salt
1-lb. can refried beans
2 1/3-2 1/2 c. Enchilada Sauce, divided (see page 63)
10 7-inch flour tortillas
Garnish: 1 c. shredded sharp Cheddar cheese

Preheat oven to 375°. In large skillet, fry beef until done; drain. Return beef to pan; add onion and garlic, then sauté until onion is translucent. Add spices and sauté 1 minute. Stir in beans and 1/4 c. Enchilada Sauce, mixing thoroughly.

Grease a 13x9-inch glass baking dish. Pour in enough Enchilada Sauce to cover bottom. Set aside.

Place filling in strip on tortilla and roll up as depicted below. Place seam side down in pan. Pour remaining Enchilada Sauce over enchiladas to cover. Cover pan with aluminum foil, then bake in preheated oven for 25-30 minutes. Remove from oven; remove foil. Top with cheese. Return to oven to melt cheese. Serves 4.

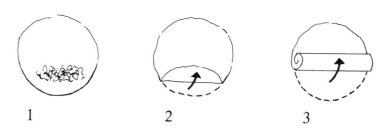

1   2   3

SAGE PORK CHOPS
WITH GREEN PEPPER SAUCE

4 pork chops
Salt and coarse black pepper
Sage
Garnish: dark green lettuce leaves
Serve with: Green Pepper Sauce (see below and
**   page 32)**

Season chops with salt and pepper. Rub sage on chops. Grill until done. Present on dark green lettuce leaf.
Serve with Green Pepper Sauce. Prepare Green Pepper Spread (see page 32), but serve hot, not chilled.
Serves 2-4.

PORK CHOPS TUSCANY

4 pork chops
Salt and coarse black pepper
1/4 c. grated Parmesan cheese
1/4 c. Italian bread crumbs
1/4 c. yellow corn meal
1 t. Italian seasoning
1/2 t. garlic salt
Vegetable oil

Season chops with salt and pepper. Combine remaining ingredients (except oil) and use to coat chops. Fry in hot oil for 30 minutes on low-to-medium heat, turning after 15 minutes. Serves 2-4.

HOPPIN' JOHN JAMBALAYA

6 smoked sausage links (I prefer Oscar Meyer)
1 T. vegetable oil
1 c. chopped onion
1/2 c. chopped green pepper
2 garlic cloves, chopped
1-lb. can blackeye peas, undrained
1 T. parsley
1/4 t. coarse black pepper
1/2 t. salt
3/4-1 c. chicken bouillon
1½ c. cooked and chilled rice, unseasoned

   Fry sausages in skillet until done. Drain and cool.
Cut into 1/2-inch thick slices. Set aside.
   Heat oil in skillet. Sauté onion, green pepper, and
garlic for approximately 5 minutes. Add sausage slices
and remaining ingredients to onion mixture. Bring to
boil, then simmer uncovered for 10 minutes. Serves 4.

RAGÙ ALLA BOLOGNESE

1 lb. ground turkey sausage
1 c. chopped onion
4 large garlic cloves, chopped (divided)
1-lb. can tomatoes, chopped and drained with juice
   reserved
1/2 c. tomato juice
8-oz. can tomato sauce
1 t. basil
1 t. oregano
1 t. sugar

1 t. parsley
1/2 t. salt
1/4 t. coarse black pepper
1 T. tomato paste
Serve with: pasta

Fry sausage in large skillet until done; drain on paper towel. Wipe out pan. Return sausage to pan. Add onion and 2 chopped garlic cloves. Sauté until onion is translucent; do not brown. Add remaining 2 chopped garlic cloves as well as other ingredients; simmer uncovered for 15 minutes on low heat. Serve over hot pasta. Serves 4.

SHRIMP CREOLE

1/3 c. butter or margarine
1 c. chopped onion
2/3-3/4 c. chopped green pepper
2 garlic cloves, chopped
1/2-3/4 t. salt
1/8 t. coarse black pepper
1 t. marjoram leaf
1-lb. can tomatoes, chopped and undrained
2/3 lb. small shrimp, boiled and drained
Serve with: rice

Melt butter in large skillet. Add onion, green pepper, and garlic, then sauté until onion is translucent. Add seasonings and tomatoes. Simmer 15 minutes, uncovered. Stir in cooked shrimp. Heat thoroughly. Serve over rice. Serves 4.

LOW COUNTRY CLAM CHOWDER

4 slices bacon
1/2 c. chopped onion
1/2 c. chopped celery
1/2 c. chopped green pepper
10 3/4-oz. can cream of potato soup
6½-oz. can minced clams, drained with liquid
  reserved
1 c. milk
Coarse black pepper

In skillet, fry bacon until crisp. Drain, then crumble when cool. Add onion, celery, and green pepper to bacon drippings in skillet. Sauté until vegetables are limp and golden; drain.

Transfer vegetables to saucepan. Add bacon, soup, reserved clam liquid, and milk. Stir to combine. Heat uncovered until hot; add clams. Heat thoroughly, but do not boil. Serves 2.

NEW ENGLAND CLAM CHOWDER: prepare as above but delete celery and green pepper.

ONION SOUP

4 medium onions, thinly sliced
1/4 c. margarine
10½-oz. can beef consommé
2/3 c. water
2 T. port
Per serving:
1 slice French bread, sliced 3/4-inch thick
1 T. Gruyère, cubed
2-3 T. shredded Gruyère
2-3 T. shredded Swiss Cheese

In large skillet, sauté onion in margarine until limp.
Cover and simmer for 15 minutes. Transfer onions to
saucepan. Add consommé, water, and port. Cover and
simmer 5 minutes. Pour soup into ovenproof individual
serving bowls, approximately three-fourths full. Place
bowls on baking sheet. Drop in cubed Gruyère, then put
1 bread slice on top of each bowl. Sprinkle shredded
cheeses over bread. Broil until cheese melts. Serves 2.

CHICKEN-CORN CHOWDER

4 slices bacon
1 medium onion, chopped
1/2 bay leaf
1 T. flour
1½ c. water
1 c. cubed potatoes (peeled)
15- or 16-oz. can cream style corn
1 c. evaporated milk
1½ t. instant chicken bouillon
1/4-1/2 t. salt
1/2 t. coarse black pepper
2 boiled chicken breasts, skinned and cubed
Garnish: fresh parsley

In skillet, fry bacon until crisp. Drain, then crumble
when cool. Pour off all but 1 T. bacon drippings from pan.
Add onion and bay leaf. Sauté until onion is translucent.
Stir in flour. Transfer onion mixture to saucepan. Add
water and potatoes; bring to a boil. Reduce heat. Cover
and simmer for 10-15 minutes. Add bacon, corn,
evaporated milk, instant chicken bouillon, salt, pepper,
and chicken. Heat until thoroughly hot. Garnish with
fresh parsley. Serve 4.

CRAB BISQUE

1/4 c. butter
6½-oz. can crabmeat, drained and cartilage removed
1 c. chicken bouillon
1 c. half-and-half
1/4-1/2 t. celery salt
2 egg yolks, beaten
2-3 drops yellow food coloring
2-3 drops red food coloring
1 T. flour, optional

Melt butter in saucepan and add crab. Sauté until heated thoroughly. Add bouillon, half-and-half, and salt. Heat on medium until hot, but do not boil. Quickly stir in egg yolks. Heat until slightly thickened. Add food colorings. Pour in batches into blender; blend until smooth. Serves 2.

If thicker bisque is desired: mix flour with 1/4 c. soup, then stir into remaining soup. Heat on stove, stirring constantly until thickened.

MINESTRONE

2 1-lb. cans great Northern beans, undrained
3 c. water
4 beef bouillon cubes
1 c. cubed potatoes (peeled)
1 c. chopped celery
1 c. chopped carrot
1 c. chopped onion

1 c. chopped zucchini
1-lb. can tomatoes, chopped and undrained
1 garlic clove, chopped
1 T. parsley
1 t. basil
Salt and coarse black pepper
Serve with: grated Parmesan cheese

Combine all ingredients in saucepan. Bring to boil. Reduce heat; cover and simmer for 30 minutes. Serve with Parmesan cheese. Serves 4.

CREAM OF PEANUT SOUP

1 c. chicken bouillon, divided
1 T. flour
1/2 c. smooth peanut butter
2 5-oz. cans evaporated milk
1/4 c. milk, optional
Salt and coarse black pepper
Garnish: chopped peanuts

In saucepan, combine 1/4 c. chicken bouillon with flour, stirring until smooth. Add remaining 3/4 c. bouillon gradually. Bring to boil; drop in peanut butter. Continue to heat, stirring until completely smooth. Reduce heat to medium; gradually add evaporated milk. Add milk, if desired. Season with salt and pepper. Heat thoroughly, then pour into mug. Garnish with chopped peanuts. Yields 4 small servings.
NOTE: I recommend serving this in a small coffee mug as an appetizer, because it is very rich and flavorful.

MANHATTAN CLAM CHOWDER

2 slices bacon
1 c. cubed potatoes (peeled)
1 c. chopped onion
1/2 c. finely chopped green pepper
1/2 c. finely chopped celery
2 c. boiling water
1-lb. can tomatoes, chopped and undrained
2 T. tomato paste
1/2 t. thyme leaf
1/2 t. salt
Coarse black pepper to taste
6½-oz. can minced clams, drained with liquid
    reserved
Garnish: fresh parsley sprigs·

In skillet, fry bacon until crisp. Drain, then crumble
when cool. Add potatoes and onion to bacon drippings in
skillet; sauté until glazed. Stir in green pepper and
celery; sauté until glazed.

Transfer mixture to saucepan. Pour in boiling water,
tomatoes, tomato paste, and seasonings. Add bacon
pieces and reserved clam liquid. Simmer uncovered for
15 minutes. Add clams and heat until hot. Garnish
serving bowl or individual serving bowls with fresh
parsley sprigs. Serves 4.

BORSCHT

1-lb. can sliced beets, drained with juice reserved
1 c. beet juice
1 c. shredded cabbage
10½-oz. can beef consommé
1/2 t. dried minced onion
1/8 t. coarse black pepper

120

2 t. sugar
1-2 t. vinegar
Garnish: sour cream

Shred beets in food processor using coarse shredder.
Combine all ingredients in saucepan. Bring to boil.
Reduce to simmer; simmer for 10 minutes uncovered.
Pour into bowl, then top with sour cream. Serves 2.

BOUILLABAISSE

1 c. chopped onion
4 large garlic cloves, chopped
1 t. olive oil
10½-oz. can chicken broth, condensed
14½-oz. can tomatoes, chopped and undrained
1/2 t. oregano
1/2 t. coarse black pepper
1/4 t. ground thyme
1/4 t. sage
1 t. parsley
1/8 t. turmeric
1 bay leaf
2 T. chopped green onion
6½-oz. can minced clams, drained with liquid
   reserved
1/2-3/4 lb. red snapper fillets, cut into 2-inch pieces
Serve with: thick slices of French bread

In stew pot, sauté onion and garlic in oil. Add chicken
broth, tomatoes, seasonings, green onion, and reserved
clam liquid. Simmer uncovered for 10 minutes. Add fish
and clams. Bring to boil then reduce to simmer. Cook
uncovered until fish begins to flake easily, about 5-7
minutes; do not overcook. Place bread slices in individual
serving bowls; ladle soup over bread. Serves 4.

GAZPACHO

2 c. chopped vine-ripened tomato (peel and core
  before chopping)
2 T. vegetable oil
3/4 c. tomato juice
1½ T. red wine vinegar
Salt and coarse black pepper
Serve with: chopped tomato, chopped cucumber,
  chopped onion, herbed croutons

Place all ingredients in blender; blend until smooth.
Season with salt and pepper; blend. Chill thoroughly.
Blend again, then serve. Top individual bowls with
combination of chopped tomato, cucumber, onion, and
croutons. Serves 2-4.

ITALIAN WHITE BEAN SOUP

4 slices bacon
2 1-lb. cans navy beans, undrained
1 c. chopped onion
2 c. water
2-3 chicken bouillon cubes
1 large garlic clove, chopped
1/4 t. garlic powder
1 t. parsley
Garnish: additional cooked and crumbled bacon

In skillet, fry bacon until crisp. Drain, then crumble
when cool. Place bacon and remaining ingredients in
saucepan. Simmer uncovered for 15 minutes. If creamier
texture is desired, mash with potato masher before serving.
Serves 3-4.

ITALIAN TUNA-EGG SALAD

6 1/8-oz. can tuna, drained and flaked
2 hard-boiled eggs, chopped
1/4 c. chopped pimiento-stuffed olives
1/4 c. finely chopped onion
1/4 t. salt
Coarse black pepper
1/4-1/3 c. salad dressing
4 medium tomatoes
Salt and coarse black pepper
Lettuce leaves

Combine tuna, eggs, olives, onion, salt, pepper, and salad dressing. Turn tomato stem side down. Cut into 6 equal wedges, cutting not quite all the way to the stem. Spread sections apart; season inside of tomato with salt and pepper. Fill each tomato with tuna salad. Serve on lettuce leaf. Serves 2-4.

ITALIAN TUNA SALAD

2 c. rainbow rotini, uncooked (also called garden
    twirls or tri-color fusilli)
6 1/8-oz. can tuna, drained and flaked
3/4 c. halved black olives, drained
3/4 c. chopped green onion
2/3-3/4 c. Italian dressing
1/4 t. coarse black pepper
1 medium garlic clove, chopped

Cook pasta until reaches al dente. Drain, then mix with other ingredients. It is important to mix while pasta is hot so that it will absorb flavors. Refrigerate at least 3 hours or overnight. Serve 3-4.

SCALOPPINI ALLA MARSALA

3 thin slices veal
Salt and coarse black pepper
Flour
3-4 T. butter
1/4 c. chicken bouillon
1/2 c. Marsala
Serve with: Risotto Milanese (see page 146)

Season veal with salt and pepper; coat with flour.
Melt butter in skillet. When hot add veal slices. Using
high heat, fry until browned, turning once. Reduce
heat to low; add chicken bouillon and cook slowly until
liquid is almost evaporated, about 2-4 minutes. Increase
heat to high; add Marsala and cook until sauce is thick,
about 2-4 minutes. Serve with Risotto Milanese. Serves 2.

CRANBERRY-AMARETTO SAUCE

1-lb. can whole berry cranberry sauce
1/4 c. Amaretto liqueur
Serve with: ham or turkey

Heat cranberry sauce in small saucepan until hot.
Add Amaretto. Stir, then serve. This sauce is also
delicious when served chilled. Yields 1 3/4 cup.

MIDWESTERN BBQ SAUCE

1 c. catsup
8-oz. can tomato sauce
1 T. vinegar
3 T. light brown sugar
1/2 t. salt
2 T. Worcestershire sauce
2 medium garlic cloves, chopped

Combine all ingredients in saucepan. Bring to boil, then reduce heat and simmer for 10 minutes, stirring constantly. This is an excellent sauce for pork or poultry. Yields 2 cups.

CARIBBEAN BBQ SAUCE

1/2 c. molasses
3 T. yellow mustard
2 T. vinegar
2 T. Worcestershire sauce
1 c. catsup

Combine all ingredients in saucepan. Heat thoroughly. This is an excellent sauce for beef. Yields 2 cups.

HORSERADISH SAUCE

8-oz. pkg. cream cheese, softened
2 T. cream style prepared horseradish
1 T. sour cream
Serve with: beef

Combine all ingredients. Serve immediately or refrigerate until serving time. Serve heated or chilled. This is an excellent sauce for beef. Yields 1 cup.

PEANUT SAUCE

1/4 c. peanut butter
1 T. soy sauce
1 t. sugar
1/3 c. water
Serve with: Oriental food

Combine all ingredients in small saucepan. Stirring constantly, heat on low until smoothly blended. Yields 1/2 cup. This is an excellent dipping sauce for Oriental food.

SIDE DISHES

SOUTHERN AMBROSIA

5 medium oranges
1 c. flaked coconut, firmly packed
2 T. confectioners' sugar
8 drained maraschino cherries, quartered

Peel oranges; cut sections into bite-size pieces. Mix with remaining ingredients. Serve immediately or chill overnight. Yields 4 cups.

INSALATA RUSSA

1½ c. cooked rice, unseasoned
1/2 c. cooked baby lima beans
1/2 c. cooked sliced carrots
1/2 c. chopped pimiento-stuffed green olives
1/2 c. chopped black olives
1/2 c. salad dressing
1 T. lemon juice
1/4 t. salt
Coarse black pepper

While vegetables are still hot, gently combine all ingredients. Chill thoroughly before serving. Serves 3-4.

SPAGHETTI SALAD

2 servings spaghetti or linguine, cooked al dente and
   drained (approximately 2 c.)
1/2 c. Italian dressing
1/4 t. garlic powder
1/4 t. coarse black pepper
1/3 c. halved black olives, well drained
14½-oz. can tomatoes, chopped and well drained
1/4 t. salt or to taste
2 c. dark green lettuce, torn into bite-size pieces
2 T. grated Parmesan cheese
Garnish: lettuce leaves

While spaghetti is still hot, toss with Italian
dressing, garlic powder, black pepper, black olives,
chopped tomatoes, and salt. Chill at least 3 hours or
overnight. Just before serving add lettuce and Parmesan
cheese. Toss, then serve in lettuce lined bowl. Serves 2-3.

INSALATA CAPRESE

Vine-ripened tomatoes
Sliced mozzarella cheese
Olive oil or vegetable oil
Fresh basil leaves
Salt and coarse black pepper

Core tomatoes, but do not peel; slice. Arrange tomatoes
and cheese slices, alternating, in rows on serving platter
or individual plates. Drizzle a small amount of oil over
salad, then garnish with fresh basil leaves. Pass salt and
pepper.

CREOLE GREEN BEAN-RED PEPPER SALAD

1-lb. pkg. frozen green beans, cooked and drained
1/2 c. chopped onion
1/2 c. chopped red pepper
1 large garlic clove, chopped
2/3 c. Italian dressing
Garnish: chopped hard-boiled egg

Combine beans, onion, and pepper in bowl. Combine garlic and dressing; pour dressing over vegetables, tossing to coat thoroughly. Cover and refrigerate at least 8 hours. Drain to serve. Garnish rim of serving dish with chopped egg. Serves 4.

SOUTHERN COLESLAW

2 T. vegetable oil
2 T. vinegar
1/4 c. sugar
1/2 t. salt
1/4 c. salad dressing
3 c. chopped cabbage
1/3 c. shredded carrot
1/4 c. chopped green pepper

Combine oil, vinegar, sugar, salt, and salad dressing. Let stand for 10 minutes.

Mix cabbage, carrot, and green pepper. Add dressing and toss. Chill at least 30 minutes before serving. Serves 3-4.

CREAM SLAW

3 c. shredded cabbage
1/3 c. chopped green onion
1/3 c. salad dressing
1 T. sugar
2 T. sour cream
Coarse black pepper
1/8 t. salt

Combine all ingredients. Refrigerate at least 5 hours before serving. Serves 3-4.

GREEN ONION-BLACK OLIVE POTATO SALAD

3 c. cubed potatoes (slightly undercooked), drained
1/4 c. Italian dressing
1/2 c. chopped green onion
1/2 c. quartered black olives
2 T. grated Parmesan cheese
1/4 t. salt
Coarse black pepper
1 medium garlic clove, chopped

While still hot, combine potatoes with remaining ingredients. Chill at least 8 hours before serving. Serves 2-3.

CARROT SALAD, ITALIAN STYLE

1½ c. shredded carrot
3-4 T. Italian dressing

Mix carrots and dressing. Serve immediately or cover and chill overnight. Serves 2.

BROCCOLI-CAULIFLOWER SALAD

2 c. broccoli flowerets
2 c. cauliflower flowerets
1/2 c. Italian dressing
1 t. chopped garlic (2-3 large garlic cloves)
1 t. basil
1/4 t. coarse black pepper
1/2 c. halved black olives, drained
Garnish: lettuce leaves

Blanche vegetables separately; drain.
Heat salad dressing in large skillet. Add garlic. Sauté on high for 1 minute. Remove pan from heat. Add basil, black pepper, black olives, and hot vegetables. Toss to coat. Cover, then refrigerate until well chilled.
Drain salad, reserving dressing. Place lettuce on serving platter or individual plates. Top with salad mixture. Drizzle with reserved dressing, if desired. Serves 4.

ITALIAN MUSTARD DRESSING

1 c. sour cream or yogurt
1 T. + 1 t. Dijon mustard
2 t. Italian salad dressing mix

Combine all ingredients. Yields 1 cup.

THOUSAND ISLAND DRESSING

2 T. vegetable oil
1/2 c. mayonnaise
3 T. catsup
1 T. sugar
2 t. vinegar

Place all ingredients in blender; blend until smooth. Dressing can be mixed with whisk or spoon, but the results will not be as smooth. Yields 3/4 cup.

ANTIPASTO SALAD

Lettuce leaves
Cherry tomatoes, halved or tomatoes, quartered
Black olives, drained
Pimiento-stuffed green olives, drained
Marinated artichoke hearts, halved and drained
Mozzarella cheese, cubed

Line a platter or individual serving plates with lettuce. Arrange other ingredients in rows on top of lettuce. Serve.

DELI SALAD

Iceberg lettuce, torn into bite-size pieces
Boston lettuce, torn into bite-size pieces
Tomato wedges
Whole black olives, well drained
Strips of mozzarella cheese
Strips of cotto salami
Serve with: Italian dressing

Mix greens in large salad bowl or in individual bowls. Arrange other ingredients on top of lettuce in groups. Serve with Italian dressing.

SPINACH-MUSHROOM SALAD

Per serving:
3 medium mushrooms
2-3 T. Italian dressing
½-1 hard-boiled egg, chopped
3 medium black olives, halved
1¼ c. fresh spinach, torn into bite-size pieces
Serve with: Italian dressing

Rinse and dry mushrooms, then thinly slice. Toss with Italian dressing. Marinate covered in refrigerator at least 30 minutes. In bowl, toss all ingredients, including marinade for mushrooms. Serve with additional Italian dressing.

BEET TOSSED SALAD

Canned sliced beets
Coarsely chopped hard-boiled egg
Iceberg lettuce, torn into bite-size pieces
Croutons (any flavor)
Chopped green onion
Serve with: favorite dressing

Drain beets, then pat dry with paper towel. Beets must be completely dry, otherwise they will discolor the lettuce. Coarsely chop beet slices. Toss with other ingredients. Serve with favorite dressing.

ARTICHOKES MEDITERRANEAN

1 T. olive oil
9- or 10-oz. pkg. frozen artichokes, cooked and
   drained
1 large garlic clove, chopped
14½-oz. can tomatoes, chopped and drained with
   juice reserved
1/2 t. oregano
1/2 t. basil
1/4 t. garlic powder
1/4 t. coarse black pepper
1-4 T. tomato juice, optional
Garnish: sliced mozzarella cheese

Heat oil in large skillet until hot. Add artichokes and garlic; sauté. Stir in tomatoes and seasonings. Heat until mixture is hot. If mixture seems dry stir in tomato juice. Grease an 11x7-inch glass baking dish. Pour mixture into dish. Top with mozzarella, then broil until cheese melts.

ARTICHOKES WITH LEMON-BUTTER SAUCE

2 fresh artichokes
1 T. vegetable oil
1 medium garlic clove
1 slice lemon or 1 T. reconstituted lemon juice
Lemon-Butter Sauce:
1/4 c. butter, melted
1 T. lemon juice, or to taste

Wash artichokes then snip off burrs with kitchen scissors. Slice bottom stem so artichokes will stand upright. Place enough water to cover artichokes in medium saucepan. Heat to boiling. Add oil, garlic, lemon, and artichokes to boiling water. Boil uncovered for 5 minutes. Cover and boil 30-35 minutes for large artichokes, 25-30 minutes for medium, and 20-25 minutes for small. Artichokes are done when leaves pull off easily. Use 2 spoons to lift artichokes out of water. Drain, then serve with sauce.

Prepare sauce: melt butter then stir in lemon juice. Serves 2.

FAVORITE "BAKED" BEANS

1-lb. can pork and beans, undrained
3 T. catsup
1 T. yellow mustard
1 medium onion, chopped
2 T. brown sugar
Garlic salt to taste

Combine all ingredients in saucepan. Cook uncovered over medium heat for 5 minutes or until thoroughly heated. Serves 4.

WESTERN BAKED BEANS

1-lb. can pork and beans, undrained
1 garlic clove, chopped
3/4 c. chopped onion
2 T. brown sugar
1 t. chili powder
1 t. dry mustard
2 T. catsup
Garnish: sliced tomato

Combine all ingredients in saucepan. Bring to boil. Reduce heat; simmer uncovered for 10-15 minutes. Spread into greased 1-qt. ceramic baking dish, then top with several tomato slices. Broil until tomatoes are heated. Serves 4.

REFRIED BEANS WITH TOMATO JUICE

1-lb. can refried beans
1/3 c. tomato juice
1 garlic clove, chopped
1 c. shredded sharp Cheddar cheese or Monterey
   Jack cheese
Garnish: sliced black olives, tortilla chips

In medium bowl, combine beans, juice, and chopped garlic. Grease a 1-qt. ceramic baking dish. Spread mixture into dish. Bake in 375° oven for 30 minutes. Remove from oven and top with cheese; sprinkle olives over cheese. Return to oven and bake until cheese melts, approximately 5 minutes. Place tortilla chips around edge of dish. Let stand 5 minutes before serving. Serves 4.

BEAN-POTATO BURRITOS

1-lb. can refried beans
2-4 T. evaporated milk (amount depends on brand of
   beans)
1/2 t. cumin
1/2 t. chili powder
1 large garlic clove, chopped
1 c. cubed potatoes (peeled), cooked and cooled
Salt and coarse black pepper
6 9-inch tortillas
Serve with: sour cream, salsa and/or picante sauce

Combine beans with other ingredients (except tortillas).
Season with salt and pepper. Use mixture to fill tortillas,
rolling up as for enchiladas (see page 112). Place seam
side down in greased 11x7-inch glass baking dish. Cover
and bake in 375° oven for 25-30 minutes. Serve with sour
cream, salsa, and/or picante sauce. Serves 4.

BROCCOLI WITH EASY CHEESE SAUCE

3 c. broccoli flowerets, cooked until tender crisp
Salt and coarse black pepper
1 t. cornstarch
5 slices American process cheese

Drain broccoli. Return to saucepan, then season
with salt and pepper. Stir in cornstarch. Tear cheese
into pieces by hand; add to broccoli. Let stand covered
on warm stove burner until cheese melts. Stir, then serve.
Serves 2.
VARIATION: cauliflower can be substituted for the
broccoli.

GERMAN STYLE RED CABBAGE

1-2 T. vegetable oil
1 medium onion, chopped
5 c. red cabbage, finely chopped
1 bay leaf
5 whole cloves
1½ c. water
6-8 T. vinegar
1 large apple, peeled, cored, and chopped
1/4 c. sugar
1/4 t. salt
1 t. cornstarch, optional

Sauté onion in oil until translucent. Add cabbage and cook until limp and oil is absorbed. Add bay leaf, cloves, water, vinegar, apple, sugar, and salt. Cover, then simmer on very low heat for 45 minutes. If necessary, thicken by sprinkling with cornstarch. Stir, then heat until liquid thickens. Remove bay leaf and cloves before serving (if you can find them). Place cabbage in serving bowl using slotted spoon. Serves 4.

DILLED CARROTS

1½ c. diagonally sliced carrots
1/4 t. dill
1/2 t. sugar
Butter
Salt to taste

Bring water to boil in small saucepan. Add carrots. Cover, then simmer until carrots are tender crisp, approximately 5-7 minutes. Drain off water. Season with dill, sugar, butter, and salt. Serves 2.

BUTTERED CELERY

1 c. water
1 chicken bouillon cube
6 celery stalks, cut into 4-inch lengths
Butter
Salt and coarse black pepper

Bring water and bouillon cube to boil. Stir to dissolve cube, then add celery. Cover and simmer until celery is tender crisp, approximately 5 minutes. Drain, then add butter. Season with salt and pepper. Serves 2-3.

EGGPLANT PARMESAN

Unpared eggplant, thinly sliced
Salt
Vegetable oil
Ragù sauce
Sliced mozzarella cheese
Grated Parmesan cheese

Lay eggplant slices on paper towel. Salt; let stand for 15 minutes. Blot surface with paper towel, then turn and repeat process.
Fry slices in hot oil (in batches) until lightly browned on both sides. Drain on paper towel. Place one layer of eggplant slices in glass baking dish. Season with salt. Pour over some ragù sauce. Top with sliced mozzarella cheese, then sprinkle with Parmesan cheese. Repeat with a second layer. Bake at 375° for 25-30 minutes. Let stand 5 minutes before serving.

BAKED POTATO DUMPLINGS

2 c. warm mashed potatoes (approximately 4 medium)
3 T. margarine or butter
Salt and coarse pepper
1 egg
2-3 T. flour
Additional flour

Place warm mashed potatoes in medium bowl. Add margarine, salt, and pepper; combine until mixture is smooth. Cool for several minutes or until comfortable enough to handle. Beat in egg and flour.

Generously grease a baking sheet. Dust hands with flour. Form mixture into 1-T. size balls. Place dumplings on sheet. Bake at 375° for 15-20 minutes or until thoroughly heated and lightly browned on bottom. Serves 2-4.

SOUTHWEST STYLE SCALLOPED POTATOES

3 T. margarine or butter
3 T. flour
1/2 t. salt
2 c. milk
4 c. sliced potatoes (approximately 4 medium)
Salt and coarse black pepper
1½ c. shredded Monterey Jack cheese
1/2 c. sliced black olives, drained

Prepare white sauce: melt margarine in saucepan. Stir in flour and salt; heat until bubbly. Remove pan from heat and add milk gradually. Return to stove and cook until thickened. Set aside.

Grease an 11x7-inch glass baking dish. Layer one-third of potatoes in dish. Season with salt and pepper, then pour over one-third of sauce. Top with one-third of cheese and one-third of olives. Beginning with potato slices, repeat process for second layer. For top layer: add remaining potato slices then season with salt and pepper; pour over sauce. Do not add cheese and olives. Bake uncovered at 350° for 30 minutes. Remove pan from oven and add remaining cheese and olives. Return to oven and bake uncovered 25-30 minutes. Let stand 5 minutes before serving. Serves 4-6.

SPANISH RICE

3¼ c. liquid (2 8-oz. cans tomato sauce + water to
equal 3¼ c. liquid)
3/4 t. salt
1 3/4 t. sugar
1 t. yellow mustard
1/4 c. margarine or butter
3/4 c. chopped green onion
3/4 c. chopped onion
1 1/3 c. rice

Bring liquid, salt, sugar, mustard, margarine, green onion, and onion to boil in medium saucepan. Stir in rice, then reduce heat. Cover and simmer for 20 minutes. Stir frequently because mixture sticks to pan bottom. Turn off heat; let stand covered on stove burner for 5 minutes. Fluff with fork, then serve. Serves 4.

FRENCH CUT GREEN BEAN CASSEROLE

1 c. chopped onion
Margarine or butter
1-lb. pkg. frozen French cut green beans, cooked and
  well drained
1/2 c. salad dressing
10 3/4-oz. can cream of chicken soup
1/2 t. coarse black pepper
Garnish: parsley

Sauté onion in margarine. Combine all ingredients.
Grease an 11x7-inch glass casserole dish. Spread mixture
into dish. Sprinkle with parsley. Bake uncovered at 350°
for 30 minutes.

PETITS POIS AUX LAITUES

2 c. iceberg lettuce, torn into bite-size pieces
2½ T. butter or margarine
10-oz. pkg. frozen green peas, thawed
1 t. sugar
1 t. parsley
1/4 t. salt
1/8 t. nutmeg

In large skillet, sauté lettuce in butter until limp.
Add peas and cook until done, approximately 5 minutes.
Stir in seasonings. Serves 3-4.

CROCCHETTE DI PATATE

2 c. mashed potatoes, cooled to room temperature
1/4 c. grated Parmesan cheese
1 egg
1/4 t. garlic powder
1/8 t. salt
Vegetable oil

Combine potatoes, cheese, egg, garlic powder, and salt. In palm of your hand, shape mixture into oblong oval shape, about 3½-inches long. Heat oil in frying pan until hot. Fry croquettes on both sides until brown. Serves 2.

ITALIAN OVEN-ROASTED POTATOES

2 medium potatoes
2 t. butter, melted
1 garlic clove, chopped
Salt and coarse black pepper

Wash potatoes, then peel. Cut as for French fries. Place potatoes in an 11x7-inch glass baking dish. Pour butter over potatoes; add garlic. Toss to coat. Bake uncovered in 375° oven for 30 minutes. Stir occasionally to prevent sticking. Season with salt and pepper before serving. Serves 2.
VARIATION: cut potatoes as for ranch fries (do not peel).

MEDITERRANEAN RICE

2½ c. water
2 t. instant chicken bouillon
2-3 T. butter or margarine
1/2 t. curry
1/2 t. turmeric
1/3 t. salt
1 c. rice
1/2 c. raisins

Bring water, bouillon, butter, curry, turmeric,
and salt to boil in medium saucepan. Stir in rice, then
reduce heat. Cover and simmer for 20 minutes, stirring
occasionally. Turn off heat. Stir in raisins. Let stand
covered on stove burner for 5 minutes. Fluff with fork
then serve. Serves 4.

LOUISIANA FIELD PEAS AND RICE

1 chicken bouillon cube
2 c. water
15- or 16-oz. can field peas, drained with liquid
    reserved
1/2 c. reserved field pea liquid
1 c. rice
1/2 t. salt
1/4 t. coarse black pepper
2 T. dried minced onion
1 T. parsley
3 T. butter or margarine

Bring chicken bouillon cube, water, and 1/2 c. reserved pea liquid to boil. Stir in rice, then reduce heat. Cover and simmer for 15 minutes, stirring occasionally. Add peas and simmer covered for additional 5 minutes. Turn off heat; stir in salt, pepper, onion, parsley, and butter. Let stand covered on stove burner for 5 minutes. Fluff with fork then serve. Serves 4.

ROJO RICE

8-oz. can tomato sauce
1½ c. water
1 medium garlic clove, chopped
1 chicken bouillon cube
1/2 t. salt
1/4 t. coarse black pepper
2 T. margarine
1 c. rice
1 c. shredded Monterey Jack cheese
1 T. canned chopped green chilies, or to taste

Bring tomato sauce, water, garlic, bouillon cube, salt, pepper, and margarine to boil in medium saucepan. Stir in rice, then reduce heat. Cover and simmer for 20 minutes, stirring occasionally. Turn off heat; let stand covered on stove burner for 5 minutes. Grease an 11x7-inch glass baking dish. Transfer rice to dish. Top with cheese, then sprinkle with chilies. Broil until cheese melts. Serves 4.

PECAN RICE

2½ c. water
1 c. rice
2/3 c. chopped pecans
1/2 c. chopped onion
2 T. margarine
1 t. salt
1/4 t. coarse black pepper
2 T. Worcestershire sauce
3/4 t. thyme leaf
1 t. sugar
1 T. parsley

In medium saucepan, bring water to boil. Stir in rice, then reduce heat. Cover and simmer for 20 minutes, stirring occasionally. In skillet, sauté pecans and onion in margarine. Add pecans and onion to cooked rice. Stir in remaining ingredients. Turn off heat. Let pan stand covered on stove burner for 5 minutes. Fluff with fork, then serve. Serves 4.

RISOTTO MILANESE

2/3 c. chopped onion
2 T. butter or margarine
2½ c. chicken bouillon
1/2 t. salt
Coarse black pepper to taste
1 c. rice
6 T. grated Parmesan cheese
Garnish: tomato wedges

In medium saucepan, sauté onion in butter until limp; do not brown. Add bouillon, salt, and pepper.

Bring to boil. Stir in rice, then reduce heat. Cover and simmer for 20 minutes, stirring occasionally. Turn off heat; let stand covered on stove burner for 5 minutes. Stir in Parmesan cheese; let stand covered on stove burner an additional 2-3 minutes. Place rice in serving bowl; garnish with tomato wedges around rim or in center of dish. Serves 4.

SPINACH-MUSHROOM CASSEROLE

10-oz. pkg. frozen chopped spinach, thawed and drained
1/2-2/3 c. undiluted cream of mushroom soup
1/2 c. sour cream
1 egg
1/4 t. coarse black pepper
1/8 t. salt
1 T. dried minced onion
Garnish: tomato slices

Combine all ingredients in medium mixing bowl. Grease a 1-quart ceramic baking dish. Spread mixture into dish. Top with tomato slices then bake in 350° oven for 30 minutes. Serves 2-3.

CHERRY TOMATO SAUTÉ

Italian dressing
Cherry tomatoes

Heat desired amount of dressing in skillet. Add cherry tomatoes. Heat until hot, stirring gently to coat. Using slotted spoon, transfer to serving bowl or use as garnish for meat platter.

ZUCCHINI JULIENNE

2 medium zucchini
1 T. butter
1 large garlic clove, chopped
Salt and coarse black pepper
Garnish: grated Parmesan cheese

Cut ends off zucchini; cut julienne style into very thin lengths. Heat butter in skillet; add zucchini and garlic. Saute' briefly. Season with salt and pepper, then transfer to serving dish. Garnish with sprinkling of Parmesan cheese. Serves 2.

ZUCCHINI WITH SOUR CREAM TOPPING

Zucchini
Salt and coarse black pepper
2 parts sour cream
1 part grated Parmesan cheese
Garnish: paprika

Trim stem off zucchini. Bring water to boil, then add zucchini. Cover and boil until tender (approximately 15 minutes); drain. Cut zucchini in half lengthwise. Place cut side up on baking sheet. Lightly season cut side of zucchini with salt and pepper.

Combine sour cream and Parmesan cheese. Spread on zucchini. Sprinkle with paprika, then broil until topping is hot.

ONION-HERB STUFFED ZUCCHINI

2 medium zucchini
1/2 c. chopped onion
Butter or margarine
1 c. coarse bread crumbs (wheat bread preferred)
1/4 c. sour cream
1/4 t. coarse black pepper
1/2 t. Italian seasoning
1 T. grated Parmesan cheese
Garnish: additional Parmesan cheese

Trim stems off zucchini, then boil, in covered medium saucepan, until tender (approximately 15 minutes). Drain.

Sauté onion in butter. In medium bowl, combine onion, bread crumbs, sour cream, black pepper, Italian seasoning, and 1 T. Parmesan cheese. Set aside.

Cut zucchini in half lengthwise. Scoop out pulp, leaving a boat shape. Measure 1/2 c. chopped pulp and add to mixing bowl. Mix, then use to fill zucchini shells.

Sprinkle each zucchini half with additional Parmesan cheese, then place on baking sheet. Bake at 375° for 25-30 minutes. Serves 2.

DESSERTS

APFELKUCHEN

Crust:
20-oz. pkg. refrigerated sugar cookie dough
Filling:
20-oz. can sliced apples, drained
1 t. cinnamon
1/8 t. nutmeg
8-oz. pkg. cream cheese, softened
1/2 c. sugar
1 egg
2 T. cornstarch
Garnish: cinnamon, confectioners' sugar

Preheat oven to 350°. Grease a 9-inch springform pan. Cut dough into 1/4-inch thick slices. Using fingers, press on bottom and halfway up sides of pan.

Drop apple slices into pan; sprinkle with cinnamon and nutmeg. Using electric mixer, beat cheese, sugar, egg, and cornstarch until smooth; pour over apples. Garnish with sprinkling of additional cinnamon. Bake for 25-30 minutes. Edge of crust will be lightly browned and the filling will be set.

Serve at room temperature. Garnish cake with sprinkling of confectioners' sugar before serving. Refrigerate leftovers. Serves 8.

ALASKA BLUEBERRY CAKE

1/4 c. margarine
2/3 c. light brown sugar, firmly packed
1¼ c. fresh or frozen blueberries (thaw berries if
    frozen)
1 c. + 2 T. flour
2 t. baking powder
1/4 t. salt
1 c. sugar
1/4 c. shortening
2/3 c. milk
1 t. vanilla
1 egg

Preheat oven to 350°. Grease sides of 9-inch square
glass baking dish; melt margarine and pour in pan;
sprinkle brown sugar over margarine, then drop in
blueberries.

In medium bowl, sift together flour, baking powder,
salt, and sugar. Add shortening, milk, and vanilla.
Mix on low speed of electric mixer for 2 minutes; add
egg; mix on low speed for 1 minute. Pour batter over
berries. Bake in preheated oven for 30-40 minutes or
until golden brown. Remove cake from oven; loosen sides
with knife then turn out onto platter. If berries
stick to pan, scrape them out and pat onto cake.
Serve at room temperature. Serves 6.

CAJUN DEVIL CAKE

Cake:
5 T. cocoa
2 c. sifted flour
1/4 t. salt
1 t. soda
1/2 t. baking powder
1½ t. cinnamon
1 c. light brown sugar, lightly packed
1/2 c. sugar
2 eggs, beaten
3/4 c. oil
1 t. vanilla
1 c. cold water, scant
Frosting:
1 c. chocolate chips, melted
1/3 c. butter, softened
1 t. dry instant coffee
1 t. vanilla
2-3 c. sifted confectioners' sugar
2-3 T. coffee, prepared

Preheat oven to 350°. Grease and flour two 9-inch cake pans.

In large bowl, combine cocoa, flour, salt, soda, baking powder, cinnamon, and both sugars. Stir in remaining ingredients. Beat with electric mixer for 2 minutes. The batter will be very thin. Pour into prepared pans. Bake in preheated oven for 20-30 minutes. Cake is done when toothpick inserted in center of cake comes out clean. Frost when completely cool.

Prepare frosting: melt chips in microwave or in double boiler. Stir in butter, beating until smooth. Dissolve instant coffee in vanilla; add to chocolate mixture. Stir in sugar. Gradually add coffee to thin. Spread on cooled cake. Achieve a glazed finish by frequently dipping your knife into hot water while frosting cake. Flavor is best when prepared a day in advance of serving. Serves 8.

TOFFEE FUDGE

Butter
1½ c. chocolate chips
12-oz. pkg. butterscotch chips
14-oz. can sweetened condensed milk
1 t. vanilla
3/4 c. chopped walnuts or pecans

Line the bottom of a 9-inch square dish with wax paper. Grease the wax paper with butter.
Partially melt chocolate and butterscotch chips in microwave or in double boiler. Stir in milk. Continue heating until chips are melted, stirring occasionally. Remove from heat source; stir in vanilla and nuts. Pour into prepared pan. Cover then refrigerate until set, approximately 2 hours. Cut into squares. Yields 2½ pounds.

CHIPPETY PEANUT BUTTER FUDGE

Butter or margarine
2 c. sugar
1 c. milk
7-oz. jar marshmallow creme
1 t. vanilla
1 c. smooth peanut butter
1/4-1/3 c. chocolate chips

Grease a 9-inch square dish with butter or margarine. In medium saucepan, combine sugar and milk. Stirring constantly, bring to boil. Reduce heat to medium. Stirring constantly, boil approximately 5 minutes or until mixture reaches soft-ball stage (234°-240°). Remove pan from heat; beat in marshmallow creme, vanilla, and peanut butter. Continue to beat until mixture is comletely smooth. Pour into prepared pan. Cool 15 minutes. Sprinkle chocolate chips over candy, then gently press chips into surface. Chill until chips are firm, then cut into squares. Refrigerate leftovers. Yields 2 pounds.

HIKER'S OR BIKER'S BIRDSEED

16-oz. pkg. M & M candy
1 c. unsalted peanuts
1 c. raisins
2 c. Life or Golden Grahams cereal (or substitute your favorite cereal)

Combine all ingredients. Place 1 c. of mixture in individual airtight bags for a hiking or biking snack. Couch potatoes like this snack, too! Yields 6 cups.

PEANUT BUTTER TRUFFLES

1 envelope nonfat dry milk (1-quart size)
1/4 c. honey
1/2 c. smooth peanut butter
3/4 c. chocolate chips (do not substitute chocolate
flavored chips)

Using hand, combine dry milk, honey, and peanut butter. Shape into 1-inch balls. Melt chips in microwave or in double boiler. Using spoon, coat half of ball with melted chocolate. Place chocolate side up on wax-paper-lined baking sheet. Chill until firm. Yields 1½ dozen.

COOKIE PIZZA

1/2 c. margarine, melted
1/2 c. sugar
1/2 c. light brown sugar, lightly packed
1 egg
1 t. vanilla
1 3/4 c. flour
1 t. soda
1/2 t. salt
1 c. chocolate chips

Preheat oven to 350°. Combine margarine and both sugars. Add egg and vanilla. Stir in flour, soda, and salt. When well combined add chips. This is a very stiff dough. Grease a 14-inch pizza pan. Using hands, pat dough into pan leaving an 1-inch border. Bake in preheated oven for 10-15 minutes or until dough is light brown. Cool 7-10 minutes. Cut into squares with sharp knife. Use spatula to loosen cookies from sheet. Yields 3 dozen.

CHRISTMAS COOKIES

1/2 c. margarine, melted
1/2 c. sugar
1/2 c. light brown sugar, lightly packed
1 egg
1 t. vanilla
1 3/4 c. + 2 T. sifted flour
1 t. soda
1/2 t. salt
1 c. chopped pecans or walnuts
3/4 c. chopped mixed candied fruit
3/4 c. chopped dates

Preheat oven to 350°. Combine margarine and both sugars. Add egg and vanilla. Stir in flour, soda, and salt. Add nuts, candied fruit, and dates. Drop dough by rounded teaspoon onto a lightly greased baking sheet. Bake in preheated oven for 7-10 minutes or until cookies are lightly browned. Yields 3 dozen.

CASHEW COOKIES

2/3 c. sugar
1 c. margarine, softened
1 t. vanilla
2 c. flour
1 c. coarsely chopped salted cashews (approximately 5 oz.)
Garnish: confectioners' sugar

Using electric mixer, cream together sugar and margarine. Add vanilla; continue to mix until light and fluffy. Add flour, mixing well. Add cashews. Cover and chill dough for 2 hours or until firm enough to handle.

Preheat oven to 375°. Shape dough into 1-inch balls. Place 1-inch apart on ungreased baking sheet. Bake in preheated oven for 12-15 minutes; do not brown. Remove cookies to paper towel. Generously sift with confectioners' sugar while still warm. Cool, then store in airtight container. Dust cookies with additional confectioners' sugar before serving. Yields 4 dozen. PECAN COOKIES: substitute pecans for cashews.

BRANNIES

1 c. All-Bran cereal (do not use Extra-Fiber All-Bran)
1 c. milk
1/2 c. sugar
2 T. vegetable oil
1 egg
1 c. flour
1/4 c. cocoa
1/2 t. salt
1 t. vanilla
**1 c. chocolate chips (do not substitute chocolate
    flavored chips)**

Preheat oven to 350°. Grease and flour a 9-inch square glass baking dish. In small bowl, combine 1 c. All-Bran and milk. Set aside to soak for 5 minutes.

In medium bowl, stir together sugar and oil; the mixture will be dry. Add egg; stir in bran-milk mixture; add flour, cocoa, salt, and vanilla. Pour into prepared pan and bake in preheated oven for 20-25 minutes. Remove pan from oven; sprinkle evenly with chips. Return to oven to melt chips, approximately 1-2 minutes. Remove from oven and spread with knife to smooth. Cool completely, then cut into squares using a hot knife.

COFFEE CHEESECAKE

Crust:
1½ c. chocolate cookie crumbs
3 T. margarine, melted
2 T. light brown sugar, firmly packed
3/4 t. dry instant coffee
1/2 t. cinnamon
Filling:
3 8-oz. pkgs. cream cheese, softened
1 c. sugar
3 eggs
3 T. Kahlúa
2 T. dry instant coffee
1 c. sour cream
Garnish: finely ground coffee beans

Grease the sides of a 9-inch springform pan. In small bowl, combine crust ingredients; press firmly onto bottom of pan.

Preheat oven to 300°. Using electric mixer, beat cheese until light and fluffy. Gradually add sugar. Add eggs one at a time, beating well after each addition. Mix Kahlúa and 2 T. instant coffee, stirring until dissolved. Add Kahlúa-coffee mixture and sour cream to batter; mix until well combined. Pour into prepared pan. Bake in preheated oven for 30-45 minutes.

Cheesecake is done when cake springs back when lightly touched in center; cheesecake will shake when removed from oven. Cool at room temperature on rack for 1 hour, then cover and chill overnight.

Garnish by sprinkling rim of cheesecake with finely ground coffee beans. Serves 10-12.

ORANGE CHEESECAKE

Crust:
1½ c. chocolate cookie crumbs
3 T. margarine, melted
Filling:
2 8-oz. pkgs. cream cheese, softened
1 c. + 2 T. sugar
2 eggs
1/4 c. orange juice concentrate, frozen and undiluted
  (use dry measuring cup)
1 T. grated orange rind
6 drops yellow food coloring
6 drops red food coloring
1 t. vanilla
1/2 c. sour cream
Garnish: 6-8 dollops of whipped cream or non-dairy
  whipped topping, chocolate syrup

Grease sides of a 9-inch springform pan. In small bowl, combine cookie crumbs and melted margarine; press firmly onto bottom of pan.

Preheat oven to 300°. Using electric mixer, beat cheese until light and fluffy. Gradually add sugar. Add eggs one at a time, beating well after each addition. Add remaining ingredients, mixing thoroughly. Pour into prepared pan. Bake in preheated oven for 25-35 minutes. Cheesecake is done when cake springs back when lightly touched in center; the cheesecake will shake when removed from oven. Cool at room temperature on rack for 1 hour, then cover and chill overnight before serving.

Garnish with 6-8 dollops of whipped cream spaced evenly around edge of cheesecake. Drizzle syrup over each dollop. Serves 8-10.

FAVORITE LIQUEUR CHEESECAKE

Graham Cracker Crust:
2 c. graham cracker crumbs
1/4 c. sugar
1/4 c. margarine, softened
Filling:
3 8-oz. pkgs. cream cheese, softened
1 c. sugar
3 eggs
3/4 c. sour cream
1/2 c. liqueur (see suggestions below)

In small bowl, combine crust ingredients; press firmly onto bottom and halfway up sides of a 9-inch springform pan.

Preheat oven to 300°. Using electric mixer, beat cheese until light and fluffy. Gradually add sugar. Add eggs one at a time, beating well after each addition. Add sour cream and liqueur; mix until well combined. Pour into prepared pan. Bake in preheated oven for 45-60 minutes. Cheesecake is done when cake springs back when lightly touched in center; cheesecake will shake when removed from the oven. Cool at room temperature on rack for 1 hour, then cover and chill overnight. Serves 10-12.

Liqueur suggestions.....
HAZELNUT CHEESECAKE: use 1/2 c. hazelnut liqueur. If desired, add 4 drops yellow food coloring and 2 drops red food coloring to the batter. Remove cheesecake from oven 5 minutes before it is done. Mix topping ingredients: 1 1/3 c. sour cream, 2 T. sugar, and 2 T. hazelnut liqueur. Spread over cheesecake. Return to oven and bake 5 minutes. Cool as directed. Garnish with whole hazelnuts around outside edge of cake.

CURAÇAO CHEESECAKE: substitute 1 c. light brown
sugar, packed, for 1 c. sugar. Use 1/2 c. Curaçao.
Add 2 t. vanilla when adding liqueur. If desired,
add 8 drops yellow food coloring and 8 drops red
food coloring. Bake and cool as directed. Garnish
center of cake with twisted orange slice and fresh
mint leaf. Sprinkle with confectioners' sugar.
PRALINE CHEESECAKE: substitute 1 c. light brown
sugar, packed, for 1 c. sugar. Use 1/2 c. praline
liqueur. Add 2 t. vanilla when adding liqueur. Pour
half of batter into prepared pan. Mix 1/3 c. chopped
pecans with 1 t. flour; sprinkle over batter. Pour
remaining batter into pan; sprinkle with additional
1/3 c. chopped pecans. Bake and cool as directed.
Present individual slices drizzled with maple syrup.
KAHLÚA CHEESECAKE: substitute 1 c. light brown
sugar, packed, for 1 c. sugar. Use 1/2 c. Kahlúa.
Add 2 t. vanilla when adding liqueur. Bake and cool
as directed. Garnish with chocolate curls (see
page 173) placed in center of cake.
GRASSHOPPER CHEESECAKE: substitute chocolate
cookie crust (see page 162) for Graham Cracker
Crust. Press onto bottom and halfway up sides of
9-inch springform pan. Use 1/4 c. + 2 T. green
crème de menthe and 3 T. white crème de cacao
instead of 1/2 c. liqueur. If desired, add 2-3
drops of green food coloring. Bake and cool as
directed. Garnish with 6-8 dollops of whipped
cream around outside edge of cheesecake. Stud each
dollop with a chocolate curl (see page 173).
IRISH CREAM CHEESECAKE: use 1/2 c. sour cream,
not 3/4 c. sour cream and 3/4 c. Irish Cream
liqueur, not 1/2 c. liqueur. Bake and cool as
directed.

OREO CHEESECAKE

Chocolate Cookie Crust:
2 c. chocolate cookie crumbs
1/4 c. margarine, melted
Filling:
3 8-oz. pkgs. cream cheese, softened
1¼ c. sugar
3 eggs
1 c. sour cream
2 t. vanilla
1½ c. coarsely broken chocolate sandwich cookies
  (I prefer Oreos)

In small bowl, combine crust ingredients; press firmly onto bottom and halfway up sides of a 9-inch springform pan.

Preheat oven to 300°. Using electric mixer, beat cheese until light and fluffy. Gradually add sugar. Add eggs one at a time, beating well after each addition. Add sour cream and vanilla; mix until well combined. Pour half of batter into prepared pan. Sprinkle with 3/4 c. broken cookies; pour remaining batter into pan; sprinkle with remaining broken cookies; pat pieces to smooth top. Bake in preheated oven for 45-55 minutes. Cheesecake is done when cake springs back when lightly touched in center; cheesecake will shake slightly when removed from oven. Cool on rack for 1 hour, then cover and chill overnight. Serves 10-12.

WHITE CHOCOLATE CHEESECAKE

Graham Cracker Crust:
1¼ c. graham cracker crumbs
2 T. sugar
3 T. margarine, softened
Filling:
3 8-oz. pkgs. cream cheese, softened
1/2 c. sugar
3 eggs
1/2 c. sour cream
2 6-oz. pkgs. Nestle Premier White Baking Bars,
  melted (Melt in heavy gauge pan over low heat,
  stirring constantly. Or, melt in microwave on
  defrost. Stop and stir frequently.)
1 T. vanilla
Garnish: Strawberry Fans (see page 168)

Grease sides of a 9-inch springform pan. In small
bowl, combine crust ingredients; press firmly onto bottom
of pan.

Preheat oven to 300°. Using electric mixer, beat
cheese until light and fluffy. Gradually add sugar, mixing
thoroughly. Add eggs one at a time, beating well after
each addition. Add sour cream, melted chocolate, and
vanilla; mix until well combined. Pour filling into
prepared pan. Bake in preheated oven for 30-40 minutes.
Cheesecake is done when cake springs back when lightly
touched in center; cheesecake will shake when removed
from oven. Cool on rack for 1 hour, then cover and chill
overnight.

Present individual slices garnished with strawberry
fans. Serves 8-10.

MILK CHOCOLATE CHEESECAKE

Graham Cracker Crust (see page 160)
Filling:
2 8-oz. pkgs. cream cheese, softened
1/2 c. sugar
2 eggs
2/3 c. sour cream
1 t. vanilla
1 c. milk chocolate chips, melted
Garnish: 8-10 Milk Chocolate Dipped Strawberries
(see page 169)

Prepare crust as directed. Press firmly onto bottom and halfway up sides of 9-inch springform pan.

Preheat oven to 300°. Using electric mixer, beat cheese until light and fluffy. Gradually add sugar. Add eggs one at a time, beating well after each addition. Add sour cream, vanilla, and melted chips; mix until well combined. Pour into prepared pan. Bake in preheated oven for 40-50 minutes. Cheesecake is done when cake springs back when lightly touched in center; cheesecake will shake slightly when removed from oven. Cool on rack for 1 hour, then cover and chill overnight.

Garnish rim of cake with Milk Chocolate Dipped Strawberries. Serves 8-10.

BAKLAVA

4 12x17-inch sheets phyllo dough
2-3 T. melted butter
Nut Filling:
1 c. coarsely chopped walnuts

2 T. sugar
1/2 t. cinnamon
Syrup:
3 T. honey
2 T. water
1 T. + 1 t. sugar
Garnish: 8 whole cloves, butter, chocolate syrup
Serve with: chocolate syrup

Preheat oven to 375°. Lay 1 sheet of dough on dry surface. Brush with butter. Place second sheet on top; brush with additional butter. Cut sheet in half lengthwise. Repeat process with remaining 2 sheets. Set aside while preparing filling.

Combine all filling ingredients. Place one-fourth of filling mixture on one end of dough half. Fold up edge over filling and fold sides inwards. Roll up as for egg roll (see page 38). Lightly grease a baking sheet with butter. Place rolls seam side down on baking sheet. Stud each roll with 2 whole cloves. Brush top of rolls with butter. Bake in preheated oven for 20 minutes or until golden brown and crisp.

Prepare syrup: combine syrup ingredients. Heat in microwave or on stove until boiling and all sugar is dissolved.

Remove rolls from oven and place on plate. Prick top of rolls with toothpick. Pour syrup over rolls; let stand to absorb syrup. When cool, store rolls in airtight container at room temperature.

To serve: heat chocolate syrup until warm. Nap individual serving plates with syrup. Place 2 rolls on each plate. Pass additional sauce. Serves 2.

PROFITEROLES

1/2 c. water
1/4 c. margarine or butter
dash of salt
1/2 c. flour
2 eggs
Chocolate sauce
Whipped cream or non-dairy whipped topping

Preheat oven to 450°. Bring water, margarine, and salt to boil in small saucepan. Add flour all at once. Stir vigorously, cooking until the mixture leaves sides of the pan and forms a ball. Remove from heat. Cool 2 minutes. Add eggs, one at a time, beating until mixture is thick and shiny. Using rounded teaspoon, drop dough 2-inches apart onto lightly greased baking sheet. Bake in preheated oven for 15 minutes. Lower heat to 350° and bake 20 minutes. Split 1 puff to check for doneness; if too doughy on the inside return to oven and bake a few more minutes. Transfer to rack and cool completely. Store in airtight container at room temperature until time to use.

To assemble: just before serving, heat chocolate sauce. Meanwhile split puffs and fill with whipped cream. Place 3-4 filled puffs on individual serving plates. Pour chocolate sauce over filled puffs. Pass remaining chocolate sauce. Serves 6-8.

FRENCH BRANDIED PINEAPPLE

1 medium pineapple
1/4 c. apricot flavored brandy

Cut crown off pineapple including enough pineapple so that the crown can stand upright. Set aside.

Cut pineapple into quarters, peel then core; discard core. Cut pulp into cubes. Toss cubes with brandy.

To serve: Place crown in center of a large platter. Place cubes around crown. Gig cubes with toothpicks. Serves 4.

APRICOTS AMARETTO

1 lb. 1-oz. can apricot halves in heavy syrup, drained
**   with syrup reserved**
1/2 c. reserved apricot syrup
1/4 c. Amaretto
Garnish: whipped cream or non-dairy whipped topping

Cut apricots into bite-size pieces. Combine with 1/2 c. reserved syrup and 1/4 c. Amaretto. Refrigerate until well chilled. Serve in individual bowls garnished with dollop of whipped cream. Serves 4.

MILK CHOCOLATE FONDUE

11½-oz. pkg. milk chocolate chips
4-6 T. milk
Dippers:
Banana chunks
Mandarin orange sections
Maraschino cherries
Pineapple chunks
Fresh strawberries, stems removed
Melon balls
Kiwi slices
Vanilla wafers

Melt chips in double boiler (do not use microwave). Add milk gradually, stirring until smooth. Divide mixture between 2 warm serving bowls. Place each bowl on an individual serving plate. Surround bowls with assorted dippers. Two people share 1 bowl. Use fondue forks to gig dippers. Serves 4.

STRAWBERRY FANS

Whole strawberries

Wash and dry strawberries. Using a sharp knife and starting at the tip of the berry, slice vertically into 4-6 equal sections, cutting not quite all the way to the stem. Fan the sections apart. Use to decorate desserts and fruit salads.

ORANGES CURAÇAO

2 c. diced orange sections
1/4 c. Curaçao
2-3 T. confectioners' sugar
Garnish: Strawberry Fans (see page 168)

Combine oranges, Curaçao and sugar. Cover and chill for 30 minutes or overnight. Garnish serving bowl or individual servings with strawberry fans. Serves 2-3.

MILK CHOCOLATE DIPPED STRAWBERRIES

20-24 medium strawberries, stem intact
1 c. milk chocolate chips, melted
2 t. shortening

Wash and dry berries. Set aside.
Melt chips and shortening in double boiler. Place berry in palm of hand, stem side down. Use spoon to coat bottom half of berry with chocolate, swirling to coat. Place stem side down on wax-paper-lined baking sheet. Chill until set.

CHOCOLATE AMARETTO MOUSSE

8-oz. pkg. cream cheese, softened
1½ c. milk, divided
4¼-oz. pkg. instant chocolate pudding
1/4 c. + 1 T. Amaretto
Garnish: whipped cream or non-dairy whipped
** topping**

Using electric mixer, beat cheese until light and
fluffy. Gradually add 1/2 c. milk, beating until
completely smooth. Add remaining ingredients; mix on
low speed for 1 minute. Spoon into individual serving
dishes or a large bowl. Cover and refrigerate until
time to serve. Garnish with whipped cream. Serves 4-6.

CHOCOLATE AMARETTO MOUSSE PIE

Chocolate Crust:
1½ c. flour
2 T. cocoa
1/4 t. salt
1/2 c. shortening
1/4 c. ice water
Chocolate Amaretto Mousse (see above)

Preheat oven to 450°. Combine flour, cocoa, and
salt. Cut in shortening with fork until mixture
resembles coarse crumbs. Pour in water, then mix with
fork until dough holds together. On lightly floured
surface, roll out dough into 9-inch circle. Place
pastry in 8-inch metal pie pan. There will be leftover
dough. Prick bottom of crust. Bake in preheated oven
for 10-15 minutes. Cool to room temperature.
Pour prepared Chocolate Amaretto Mousse into crust.
Cover and chill until set. Serves 6.

CREAMY LEMON MOUSSE

8-oz. pkg. cream cheese, softened
3/4 c. sugar
1/4 c. fresh lemon juice
5-6 drops yellow food coloring
1 t. grated lemon rind
8-oz. non-dairy whipped topping

Using electric mixer, beat cheese until light
and fluffy. Add sugar, lemon juice, food coloring, and
grated lemon rind. Mix thoroughly. Gently fold in
whipped topping. Spoon into individual serving dishes or
a large bowl. Cover and refrigerate until well chilled,
approximately 2 hours. Serves 6.

CHOCOLATE LEAVES

Nonpoisonous leaves (rose, lemon, geranium, gardenia,
** grape, magnolia, nasturtium, or violet)**
Semisweet chocolate squares, semisweet chocolate chips,
** milk chocolate bar, or milk chocolate chips**

Wash leaves and pat dry. Melt chocolate. Using a
pastry brush or knife tip, spread the chocolate 1/8-inch
thick on the underside of the leaf. Chocolate should be
spread almost to the edge, but not touching the edge.
Avoid getting chocolate on the front side of the leaf.
Place coated leaves on a wax-paper-lined plate. Refrigerate until firm. Remove from refrigerator and carefully
pull off leaf. Store covered in refrigerator until
time to use. Use to decorate desserts.

CHOCOLATE CHIP PIE

1/2 c. butter, melted
1/2 c. sugar
1/2 c. light brown sugar, firmly packed
1 T. Kahlúa or 1 t. vanilla
1 egg
1 1/3 c. sifted flour
1/4 t. salt
1 c. chocolate chips
1/2 c. chopped walnuts or pecans
Serve with: ice cream, chocolate syrup

Preheat oven to 325°. Grease and flour a 9-inch metal pie pan. Set aside.

Combine melted butter and both sugars; add Kahlúa and egg. Stir in flour and salt, then add chips and nuts. Spread batter into pan. Bake in preheated oven for 30-35 minutes. Pie is done when filling is set and top is golden brown. The interior texture of the cooked pie is like a moist soft cookie, very similar to the texture of fudgey brownies. Cool 15 minutes, then cut into wedges to serve. Delicious topped with ice cream and chocolate syrup. Serves 6-8.

LINZERTORTE

Crust:
20-oz. pkg. refrigerated sugar cookie dough
Filling:
1/2 c. raspberry preserves
1/2 c. strawberry preserves
1 T. water
1/2 t. almond extract
1/2 c. sliced almonds, divided

Preheat oven to 350°. Grease a 10-inch ceramic pie pan. Cut two-thirds of cookie dough into 1/8-inch thick slices. Place the cookie slices in the pan, pressing with flour-coated fingers to fit. Set aside.

Combine preserves, water, and extract. Spread mixture evenly over cookie dough. Sprinkle with 1/4 c. sliced almonds.

Form remaining cookie dough into ball then roll out into a 9-inch circle on a generous flour-coated surface. The dough will be thin. Cut into lattice strips 1/2-inch wide. Arrange lattice on top of filling. Firmly press lattice strips onto the side crust. Sprinkle with remaining 1/4 c. sliced almonds. If desired, cover edge of crust with aluminum foil strip to prevent excessive browning. Bake in preheated oven for 25-30 minutes or until crust is lightly browned (remove strip after 10-15 minutes).

CHOCOLATE CURLS

Semisweet chocolate squares, semisweet chocolate chips, or milk chocolate bar

Melt chocolate. Construct a small rectangular container using aluminum foil (double fold). Make the rectangle as wide as your vegetable peeler. Pour melted chocolate into container. Place in refrigerator several minutes to firm. Peel down sides of container. Using long strokes, pull the peeler diagonally across the chocolate (if the chocolate is not firm enough it will be mushy; if the chocolate is too firm the shavings will be brittle. Adjust temperature of chocolate by returning to refrigerator or placing in warm oven). Carefully insert a toothpick into the curl and place it on a wax-paper-lined plate. Store covered in refrigerator until time to use. Use to decorate desserts.

MENUS

The following menus are included to assist in meal planning and to stimulate your imagination.

Many of the menus feature a three-course meal consisting of an appetizer, main dish with side dishes, and a dessert. I do not prepare elaborate three-course meals everyday, but I love to prepare then occasionally. An elegant meal is such a delightful way to celebrate a special occasion, and it can brighten up even the gloomiest of days.

BRUNCH
(* Recipe given)

Melon Wedges wrapped with Sliced Ham
Uova 'mpriatorio (Eggs in Hell)*
Crocchette di Patate (Potato Croquettes)*
Hard Rolls and Butter
Orange Cheesecake*
Coffee with Espresso Topping*

Huevos Rancheros* on Tortilla or Rice
Refried Beans with Tomato Juice*
Oranges Curaçao*
Cornbread

Grillades*
Grits
Fried Eggs
Cornbread
Southern Ambrosia*

Spiced Pecans* and Orange Juice
Pain Perdu* and Syrup
Sausages
Cottage Cheese served with Strawberries
Karol's Cinnamon Coffee*

Champagne
Zippy BBQ Steak* and Fried Eggs
Cheese Scones*
Fresh Strawberries and Whipped Cream

174

LUNCH

Cheese Cubes gigged with Black Olives
Minestrone Soup* or Italian White Bean Soup*
Breadsticks wrapped with Sliced Ham
Tossed Salad and Dressing
Apricots Amaretto* and Whipped Cream

Camembert Cheese & Crackers
Pissaladière*
Tossed Salad and Dressing
French Brandied Pineapple*

Stromboli* (Pizza Turnovers)
Tossed Salad and Dressing
Ice Cream Sundaes

Gouda Cheese & Crackers
Italian Tuna Salad*
Rolls and Butter
Tossed Salad and Dressing
Cashew Cookies*

Nippy Cheese Canapés*
Low Country Clam Chowder*, New England Clam
  Chowder* or Chicken-Corn Chowder*
Southern Coleslaw*
Rolls and Butter
Chocolate Date-Nut Bread*

Tomatoes stuffed with Italian Tuna-Egg Salad*
Tossed Salad and Dressing
Milk Chocolate Dipped Strawberries*

DINNER

Grilled Salmon or Grilled Halibut served with Deluxe
  Tartar Sauce*
Tossed Salad and Dressing
Western Baked Beans*
Sourdough Rolls and Butter
Alaska Blueberry Cake*

Chicken Curry*
Assorted Condiments: Nuts, Coconut, Raisins, Chopped
  Cooked Bacon, Chutney
Rice
French Cut Green Beans
Toffee Fudge*

175

Quick Paté*
Chicken Marengo*
Rice
Petits Pois Aux Laitues (Peas with Lettuce)*
Chocolate Amaretto Mousse Pie*

Mushroom-Almond Paté* and French Bread
Coq au Vin*
Rice
Tossed Salad and Dressing
Rolls & Butter
Coffee Cheesecake*

Cheesy Smoked Walnuts*
South-of-France Cornish Hen*
Artichokes Mediterranean*
Wild Rice
Crusty Rolls and Butter
Milk Chocolate Cheesecake*

Wurst Bites* and Mustards
Rouladen*
Baked Potato Dumplings*
Buttered Green Beans
Apfelkuchen*

Bagna Cauda* and Crisp Raw Vegetables
Bistecca alla Pizzaiola*
Italian Oven-Roasted Potatoes*
Zucchini with Sour Cream Topping*
Rolls and Butter
Apricots Amaretto* & Whipped Cream

Insalata Caprese*
Spaghetti alla Carbonara*, Spaghetti all'Amatriciana*, or
    Manicotti*
Tossed Salad and Dressing
French Bread and Butter
Profiteroles*

Italian Cheeseball* and Crackers
Italian Baked Cornish Hen*
Spaghetti Salad*
Zucchini Julienne*
Creamy Lemon Mousse*

Refried Bean Dip* with Tortilla Chips
Chili Chicken*
Corn on the Cob with Butter
Beet Tossed Salad* and Dressing
Kahlúa Cheesecake*

Mexican Cheeseball* and Crackers
Roast Beef with Enchilada Sauce*
Tossed Salad and Dressing
Refried Beans
Tortillas
Curaçao Cheesecake*

Artichokes with Lemon-Butter Sauce*
Shish Kabob*
Mediterranean Rice*
Tossed Salad with Dressing
Chocolate Amaretto Mousse*

Cheesy Smoked Peanuts*
Cantonese Egg Rolls*
Chicken Fried Rice*
Tossed Salad and Dressing
Pecan Cookies*

Chicken Gumbo with Smoked Sausage*
Rice
Tossed Salad with Thousand Island Dressing*
Cornbread and Butter
Grasshopper Cheesecake*

Dill Dip* with Crisp Raw Vegetables
Shrimp Creole*
Rice
Buttered Broccoli or Green Beans
Cajun Devil Cake*

Chicken Piquant*
Louisiana Field Peas and Rice*
Tossed Salad and Dressing
Praline Cheesecake*

Shrimp Log* and Crackers
Creole Mustard Steak*
Tossed Salad with Thousand Island Dressing*
Pecan Rice*
Grasshopper Frappé*

Quesadillas*
Grilled Chicken and Salsa*
Rojo Rice*
Tossed Salad and Dressing
Santa Fe Frappé*

Crushed-Crouton Breaded Fish* and Tartar Sauce*
Corn on the Cob and Butter
Southern Coleslaw*
Platter of Sliced Tomato garnished with Black Olives
Chocolate Chip Pie* with Ice Cream and Chocolate Sauce

Maryland Crab Cakes*
Baked Potato and Butter
Cream Slaw*
Rolls and Butter
Milk Chocolate Fondue* with Dippers

Liptauer Cheese Spread* on Rye Bread
Chicken Paprika*
Buttered Noodles
Green Beans or Brussels Sprouts
Rolls and Butter
Linzertorte*

Taramosalata*
Sage Pork Chops with Green Pepper Sauce*
Baked Potato with Sour Cream
Buttered Carrots
Baklava*

HOLIDAY

New Year's Day

Hoppin' John Jambalaya*
Green Beans with Pimiento Garnish
Rolls and Butter
Pecan Ice Cream and Caramel Sauce

Easter

"Smoked" Salmon Spread* and Crackers
Ham Wellington*
Cranberry-Amaretto Sauce*
Baked Sweet Potato
Buttered Green Beans or Broccoli
Rolls and Butter
Creamy Lemon Mousse*

Fourth of July

Blue Cheese Dip* and Crisp Raw Vegetables
Grilled Chicken with Midwestern BBQ Sauce*
Corn on the Cob with Butter
Spinach-Mushroom Salad*
Oreo Cheesecake*

Thanksgiving

Pimiento Cheeseball* and Crackers
Roast Turkey Breast with Dressing
Buttered Celery*
Baked Sweet Potato and Butter
Cranberry-Amaretto Sauce*
Sweet Wheaty Biscuits* and Butter
Pumpkin Pie

Christmas

Shrimp Log* and Crackers
Roast Duck with Raisin-Raspberry Sauce*
Buttered Broccoli
Mashed Potatoes
Rolls and Butter
White Chocolate Cheesecake*

New Year's Eve

Parmesan Popcorn*
Roast Beef served with Horseradish Sauce*
Yorkshire Pudding*
Baked Potato with Sour Cream
Dilled Carrots*
Hazelnut Cheesecake*

COPING
WITH PROBLEMS

Consulting a guidebook before going on a trip is a sound idea. It prepares you for your adventure by suggesting what to see and alerts you to the pecularities of the area and how to cope with them.

Just as a good guidebook prepares you for a trip, this chapter will prepare you for possible cooking problems that you might encounter. It offers practical advice for dealing with high altitude, humidity, and extreme dryness.

A traveling cook experiences more challenges than a stationary cook. Being informed enables you to face those challenges with confidence.

DRYNESS

Arid desert air can quickly dry out your ingredients and prepared foods. Prevent dryness by taking the following precautionary measures:

- Use an airtight container for all items stored at room temperature.
- Store loaf/sandwich bread in the refrigerator or a cooler.
- Place an apple slice or slice of bread in your brown sugar container. Seal tightly, then store in the refrigerator or a cooler.

- Double bag items that you package for the freezer.
- Place an apple slice or a damp paper towel in containers storing home baked goods (cakes, cookies, breads, etc.) that are stored at room temperature.
- Rice requires additional liquid when prepared in dry climates. Watch carefully to avoid evaporation.

HUMIDITY

A damp climate can be annoying as well as physically uncomfortable. The excessive moisture causes crackers to get soggy, bread to mildew, and bugs to proliferate. The following tips will help to minimize these problems:

- Place all foods stored at room temperature in airtight containers.
- Crisp soggy crackers by baking in 275° oven for 20-30 minutes.
- Store loaf/sandwich bread in the refrigerator or a cooler to prevent mildew.
- Prevent bugs/worms from developing in your flour, cereal, and rice by wrapping the package in plastic wrap, then freezing for 24 hours. Thaw without opening.
- Avoid bugs by keeping your food preparation area as clean and dry as possible.
- Increase the cooking time to compensate for the extra moisture when making candy.

HIGH ALTITUDE

When preparing foods at high altitude (altitudes greater than 3000 feet), adjustments must be made to compensate for the lower boiling temperature and the reduced air pressure. Foods that are boiled and foods containing leavening ingredients are the major concerns.

Boiling

Water boils at 212° at sea level. As altitude increases, the boiling temperature drops (about 1° for each 500-foot increase). In other words, a boiling liquid at 5000 feet is not as hot as a boiling liquid at 3000 feet. Since it is heat that cooks food, not "boiling," compensate for the lower temperature by increasing the cooking time. And, since evaporation will be increased, more liquid may be required.

For example, at 3000 feet I simmer stew for 2½ hours, but at 5000 feet it might take 3 hours. Experimentation will determine the correct cooking time and if additional liquid should be added.

Candy preparation is an exception. Because evaporation increases at high altitudes, it will become too con-centrated and "sugary" if cooked longer. It will reach soft ball stage, hard ball stage, etc., faster than it will at normal altitude.

Unfortunately, there is not an exact formula to follow. Experimentation will yield the best results.

Leavening

Atmospheric pressure decreases as altitude increases. Essentially, this means that as air becomes thinner, foods containing leavening ingredients will rise faster and more easily.

Recipes containing yeast as a leavening agent do not require adjustment. However, they will take less time to rise than at normal altitude.

If baking powder or baking soda is used, adjustments need to be made. The chart below contains general guidelines which will prove helpful. When two amounts are listed, try the smaller amount first. If your recipe uses both baking powder and baking soda, reduce both ingredients. However, in recipes which use baking soda, never reduce below one-half teaspoon for every cup of sour milk.

When baking cakes and non-yeast breads, increase the oven temperature 25°. The higher heat stabilizes the batter and prevents falling.

Adjustment	3,000 feet	5,000 feet	7,000 feet
Reduce baking powder/ baking soda. For each teaspoon, decrease:	1/8 t.	1/8-1/4 t.	1/4 t.
Reduce sugar. For each cup, decrease:	0-1 T.	0-2 T.	1-3 T.
Increase liquid. For each cup, add:	1-2 T.	2-4 T.	3-4 T.
Increase flour. For each cup, add:	0-1 T.	1-2 T	2-3 T.

(Table courtesy of Cooperative Extension Service of New Mexico State University)

SUBSTITUTIONS/ EQUIVALENTS

SUBSTITUTIONS

Substitutions are a fact of life when camping. Although seldom as satisfactory as the original ingredient, they do enable you to prepare the recipe. Regardless of whether you are miles away from a store or it is just not convenient to shop, the following list of substitutions/equivalents will prove invaluable.

BAKING

1 c. self-rising flour	1 c. flour, 1 t. baking powder, and 1/2 t. salt
biscuit mix	5 c. flour, 1/4 c. sugar, 2 T. plus 2 t. baking powder, 1½ t. salt, and 1 c. shortening (Combine dry ingredients then cut in shortening with fork until mixture is crumbly. Store in refrigerator in air-tight container. Yields 6 cups.)
1 t. baking powder	1/4 t. baking soda plus 1/2 t. cream of tartar

DAIRY

1 c. buttermilk	1 c. milk plus 1 T. vinegar or lemon juice (Mix, then let stand at room temperature for 5 minutes.)

2 c. whipped cream (1 c. heavy cream, unwhipped)	2 c. non-dairy whipped topping
1 c. heavy cream, unwhipped	3/4 c. whole milk plus 1/3 c. butter, melted
1 c. light cream (half-and-half)	7/8 c. whole milk plus 3 T. butter, melted
1 c. whole milk	1/2 c. water plus 1/2 c. evaporated milk or 1 c. skim milk plus 2 T. butter
1 c. skim milk	4 T. nonfat dry milk plus 1 c. water
1 c. sour cream	1 c. heavy cream plus 1 T. lemon juice or vinegar (Stir together, then let stand at room temperature for 30-60 minutes to thicken. Store in refrigerator.)
14-oz. can sweetened condensed milk	1 c. nonfat dry milk, 3/4 c. sugar, 1/3 c. boiling water, and 1 T. butter (Place ingredients in blender. Blend for 5 minutes or until thick and smooth. Store in refrigerator.)

CHOCOLATE

1-oz. square unsweetened chocolate	3 T. cocoa plus 1 T. shortening or margarine
6-oz. pkg. semisweet chocolate chips, melted	2 oz. unsweetened chocolate, melted, 7 T. sugar, and 2 T. shortening, melted
3 oz. semisweet chocolate	1/2 c. semisweet chocolate chips

185

SPICES/HERBS

1 T. chopped fresh herb (parsley, basil, chives, oregano, etc.)	1 t. dry leaf herb
1 T. yellow mustard	1 t. dry mustard
1 t. Italian seasoning	1/4 t. each: thyme, oregano, basil, and marjoram
1/8 t. red cayenne pepper	4 drops Tabasco
1 garlic clove	1/8 t. garlic powder or 1/8 t. dried minced garlic
1 T. minced fresh ginger	1/4 t. ground ginger
1/4 c. chopped onion	1 T. dried minced onion

MISCELLANEOUS

1 anchovy fillet	1/2 t. anchovy paste
1/2 lb. fresh mushrooms	6-oz. can mushrooms, drained
2 c. tomato sauce	6-oz. can tomato paste plus 1½ c. water
1 c. tomato juice	1/2 c. tomato sauce plus 1/2 c. water
1 c. catsup	8-oz. can tomato sauce, 1/2 c. sugar, and 2 T. vinegar (Combine all ingredients, then heat until sugar is dissolved and mixture thickens.)
1 T. cornstarch (used as thickening agent in cooked sauces)	2 T. flour

METRIC EQUIVALENTS

Grocery shopping in Canada and Mexico can be confusing if you are unfamiliar with metric equivalents. And, if you buy a cookbook while on your trip, converting metric recipes can be difficult. The following list of equivalents will assist in your shopping and cooking.

LIQUID
(Note: most liquid measuring cups show both ounces and milliliters.)

1/4 teaspoon	1.25 milliliter
1 teaspoon	5 milliliters
1 tablespoon	15 milliliters
1/4 cup	60 milliliters
1/3 cup	80 milliliters
1 cup	250 milliliters
1 pint	500 milliliters
1 quart	.95 liter
2.1 pint	1 liter
1 gallon	3.8 liter

WEIGHT
(meats, vegetables, cheese, butter)

1 ounce	30 grams
1/4 pound	115 grams
1/2 pound	225 grams
1 pound	450 grams
2 ¼ pound	1 kilogram

SUGAR

1 teaspoon	4 grams
1 tablespoon	12 grams
1/4 cup	50 grams
1/3 cup	65 grams
1/2 cup	95 grams
1 cup	190 grams

UNSIFTED FLOUR

1 tablespoon	8.5 grams
1/4 cup	35 grams
1/3 cup	45 grams
1/2 cup	70 grams
1 cup	140 grams

OVEN TEMPERATURES

300°F = 150°C (slow)
325°F = 160°C (moderately slow)
350°F = 180°C (moderate)
375°F = 190°C (moderately hot)
400°F = 200°C (hot)
425°F = 220°C (hot)
450°F = 230°C (very hot)
500°F = 260°C (extremely hot)

BIBLIOGRAPHY

Cooperative Extension Service of New Mexico State University."High Altitude Cooking." Las Cruces: New Mexico State University. 1981.

Groene, Janet. COOKING ON THE GO. New York: Hearst Marine Books. 1987.

Hoffman, Mildred. CHOCOLATE COOKERY. Tucson: H.P. Books. 1978.

Patterson, Monita, ed. PASSING THROUGH KOREA: AMERICAN WOMEN'S CLUB COOKBOOK. Seoul, Korea: American Women's Club. 1987.

Rombauer, Irma S. & Marion Rombauer Becker. JOY OF COOKING. New York: Bobbs-Merrill Company, Inc. 1980.

Ying, Mildred, ed. THE NEW GOOD HOUSEKEEPING COOKBOOK. New York: Hearst Books. 1986.

INDEX

A

Alaska Blueberry Cake, 151
Almond Crusted Fish, 103
Ambrosia, Southern, 127
Antipasto Salad, 132
Apfelkuchen, 150
Appetizers
  Cheeseballs
    Italian, 29
    Mexican, 30
    Pimiento, 30
  Dips
    Bagna Cauda, 31
    Blue Cheese, 32
    Chile con Queso, 27
    Dill, 28
    Refried Bean, 26
    Salsa, 31
    Taramosalata, 28
  Egg
    Mexican Style
      Deviled Eggs, 37
  Hot
    Arizona Cheese Crisp, 34
    Cantonese Egg Rolls, 38
    Nippy Cheese Canapés, 34
    Quesadillas, 35
    Wurst Bites, 37
  Nuts
    Cheesy Smoked Peanuts, 36
    Cheesy Smoked Walnuts, 36
    Spiced Pecans, 36
  Paté
    Mushroom-Almond Paté, 25
    Quick Paté, 26
  Popcorn
    Parmesan Popcorn, 35
  Spreads
    Green Pepper, 32
    Liptauer Cheese, 29
    Red Pepper, 32
    Shrimp Log, 33
    "Smoked" Salmon, 33
Apple Pancakes, 54

Apricots Amaretto, 167
Arizona Cheese Crisp, 34
Artichokes
  with Lemon-Butter
    Sauce, 135
  Mediterranean, 134

B

Bacon
  Spaghetti all'Amatriciana, 61
  Spaghetti alla Carbonara, 60
Bagna Cauda, 31
Baked
  "Blackened" Chicken, 86
  Chicken Pecan, 84
  Fish, Italian Style, 99
  Potato Dumplings, 140
Baklava, 164
Banana Daiquiris, 39
Basic Omelet, 96
Basic Pantry, 10-16
Bean-Potato Burritos, 137
Beans, Baked
  Favorite, 135
  Western, 136
Beans, Refried
  Bean-Potato Burritos, 137
  Dip, 26
  with Tomato Juice, 136
Beef
  Bistecca alla
    Pizzaiola, 70
  Carne Asada, 69
  Creole Mustard Steak, 65
  Grillades, 66
  Ground, see ground beef
  Herb Marinated Steak, 72
  and Peppers, 71
  Roast
    Cajun, 65
    with Enchilada Sauce, 63
    Marinated, 64
  Rouladen, 62
  Shish Kabob, 68

189

Steak Waikiki,67
Stroganoff,73
Teriyaki Steak, 67
Zesty Steak Salad, 70
Zippy BBQ Steak, 72
Beef and Bean Enchiladas, 112
Beets
Borscht, 120
Tossed Salad, 134
Beverages
Banana Daiquiris, 39
Espresso Topping for
Coffee, 42
Gluehwein, 42
Grasshopper Frappé, 40
Karol's Cinnamon
Coffee, 41
Mexican Hot
Chocolate, 41
Mulled Cranberry-Port, 43
Santa Fe Frappé, 40
Spirited Café Mocha, 41
Strawberry Daiquiris, 39
Velvet Hammer Frappé, 40
Bird of Paradise Chicken
Salad, 82
Birdseed, 154
Biscuits
Cheese Scones, 44
Raisin Scones, 45
Sweet "Rolls", 46
Sweet Wheaty, 44
Bistecca alla Pizzaiola, 70
Blue Cheese
Dip, 32
Salad Dressing, 32
Blueberry
Alaska Blueberry Cake, 151
Syrup, 54
Borscht, 120
Bouillabaisse, 121
Bourbon-Apple Coffeecake, 52
Brannies,157
Bread
Chippety Chocolate, 49
Chocolate Date-Nut, 47
Chocolate Raisin Zucchini, 48
Wholesome Wheat Beer, 50
Yorkshire Pudding, 55

Broccoli
Cauliflower Salad, 131
with Easy Cheese Sauce, 137
Stir-Fry Chicken with
Broccoli, 85
Broiled Salmon
with Creamy Herb Sauce, 104
with Parmesan Topping, 103
Buttered Celery, 139

C

Cajun
Devil Cake, 152
Roast Beef, 65
Cake
Alaska Blueberry, 151
Apfelkuchen, 150
Cajun Devil, 152
California Style Chicken
Salad, 82
Candy
Chippety Peanut
Butter Fudge, 154
Hiker's or Biker's
Birdseed, 154
Peanut Butter
Truffles, 155
Toffee Fudge, 153
Cantonese Egg Rolls, 38
Caribbean BBQ Sauce, 125
Carne Asada, 69
Carrots
Dilled, 138
Salad, Italian
Style, 131
Cashew Cookies, 156
Catfish, Lemon-Dill, 100
Cauliflower
Broccoli-Cauliflo-
wer Salad, 131
with Easy Cheese Sauce, 137
Celery, Buttered, 139
Cheddar Tart, 98
Cheese Scones, 44
Cheeseballs, see
appetizers
Cheesecake
Coffee, 158

Curaçao, 161
Favorite Liqueur, 160
Grasshopper, 161
Hazelnut, 160
Irish Cream, 161
Kahlúa, 161
Milk Chocolate, 164
Orange, 159
Oreo, 162
Praline, 161
White Chocolate, 163
Cheesy Smoked
Peanuts, 36
Walnuts, 36
Cherry Tomato Sauté, 147
Chicken
Baked "Blackened", 86
Baked Chicken Pecan, 84
Bird of Paradise
Salad, 82
Cacciatora, 80
California Style Salad, 82
Chili Chicken, 78
with Chutney Sauce, 75
Coq au Vin, 81
Corn Chowder, 117
Curry, 87
Double-Bar Ranch BBQ, 78
Fried Rice, 86
Gumbo with Smoked
Sausage, 88
Italian Style Roast, 79
Marengo, 79
Northern Fried, 83
Paprika, 76
Pecan, 84
Pepper Kabobs, 84
Piquant, 74
Pollo alla Forno, 80
Pot Pie, 77
Roast, Italian Style, 79
Southern Fried, 83
Stir-Fried
with Broccoli, 85
with Lettuce, 89
Chile con Queso, 27
Chili, 108
Chili Chicken, 78

Chippety
Chocolate Bread, 49
Peanut Butter Fudge, 154
Chocolate
Amaretto Mousse, 170
Amaretto Mousse Pie, 170
Cajun Devil Cake, 152
Chippety Chocolate Bread, 49
Curls, 173
Date-Nut Bread, 47
Leaves, 171
Mexican Hot Chocolate, 41
Milk Chocolate
Cheesecake, 164
Dipped Strawberries, 169
Fondue, 168
Raisin Zucchini Bread, 48
White Chocolate
Cheesecake, 163
Chocolate Chip Pie, 172
Chowder
Chicken-Corn, 117
Low Country Clam, 116
Manhattan Clam, 120
New England Clam, 116
Christmas
Cookies, 156
Toast, 94
Clam
Low Country Chowder, 116
Manhattan Chowder, 120
New England Chowder, 116
White Clam Sauce, 90
Coffee
Cheesecake, 158
Espresso Topping, 42
Karol's Cinnamon, 41
Kuchen, 51
Spirited Café Mocha, 41
Coffeecake
Bourbon-Apple, 52
Coffee Kuchen, 51
Rum-Raisin, 52
Strawberry Breakfast
Cake, 53
Coleslaw
Cream, 130
Southern, 129

Cookies
  Brannies, 157
  Cashew, 156
  Christmas, 156
  Pecan, 157
  Pizza, 155
Coq au Vin, 81
Cornish Hen
  Italian Baked, 90
  South-of-France, 91
Crab
  Bisque, 118
  Maryland Crab Cakes, 92
Cranberry-Amaretto Sauce, 124
Cream of Peanut Soup, 119
Cream Slaw, 130
Creamy
  Herb Sauce, 104
  Lemon Mousse, 171
Creole
  Butter Sauce, 98
  Green Bean-Red Pepper
    Salad, 129
  Mustard Steak, 65
  Sauce, 66
  Shrimp, 115
Crocchette di Patate, 143
Crushed-Crouton Breaded
  Fish, 99
Curaçao Cheesecake, 161

D

Daiquiris,
  Banana, 39
  Strawberry, 39
Deli Salad, 133
Deluxe
  Apple Pancakes, 54
  Pecan Pancakes, 54
  Tartar Sauce, 105
Dill Dip, 28
Dilled Carrots, 138
Dips, see Appetizers
Double-Bar Ranch BBQ
  Chicken, 78
Dryness, 180, 181
Duck, Roast with Raisin-
  Raspberry Sauce, 92

E

Easy
  Cheese Omelet, 96
  Cheese Sauce, 137
  Tartar Sauce, 104
Egg Rolls, Cantonese, 38
Eggplant Parmesan, 139
Eggs
  Basic Omelet, 96
  Cheddar Tart, 98
  Christmas Toast, 94
  Easy Cheese Omelet, 96
  Enchilada, 93
  Green Chili Quiche, 95
  in Hell, 95
  Herb Omelet, 96
  Huevos Rancheros, 97
  Italian Tuna-Egg Salad, 123
  Mexican Style Deviled, 37
  Monterey Omelet, 96
  Muenster Tart, 98
  Pain Perdu, 94
  Scrambled with Mushroom, 97
  Uova 'mpriatorio, 95
  Western Omelet, 96
Enchilada Sauce, 63
Enchiladas
  Beef and Bean, 112
  Egg, 93
Equipment, 18-21
Equivalents, 184-187
Espresso Topping for
  Coffee, 42

F

Favorite
  "Baked" Beans, 135
  Liqueur Cheesecake, 160
Fish
  Almond Crusted Fish, 103
  Baked, Italian Style, 99
  Bouillabaisse, 121
  Broiled Salmon with
    Creamy Herb Sauce, 104
  Parmesan Topping, 103
  Creole Butter Sauce, 98
  Crushed-Crouton
    Breaded, 99

192

Deluxe Tartar Sauce, 105
Easy Tartar Sauce, 104
Herbed Fishwiches, 101
Hickory BBQ, 100
Italian-Breaded Fried
 Trout, 102
"Just for the Halibut"
 Burgers, 105
Lemon-Dill Catfish, 100
Mustard Butter Sauce, 101
Spanish Sauce, 102
Frappé
 Grasshopper, 40
 Santa Fé, 40
 Velvet Hammer, 40
French Brandied Pineapple, 167
French Cut Green Bean
 Casserole, 142
Fried Chicken
 Northern, 83
 Southern, 83
Frittata, 111
Fudge
 Chippety Peanut Butter
  Fudge, 154
 Toffee, 153

G

Gazpacho, 122
German Style Red Cabbage, 138
Gluehwein, 42
Grasshopper
 Cheesecake, 161
 Frappé, 40
Green Bean-Red Pepper
 Salad, Creole, 129
Green Chili Quiche, 95
Green Onion-Black Olive
 Potato Salad, 130
Green Pepper
 Sauce, 32
 Spread, 32
Grillades, 66
Ground beef
 Beef and Bean Enchiladas, 112
 Chili, 108

Frittata, 111
Italian Meatballs, 110
Italian Meatloaf, 109
Italian Submarine
 Sandwich, 111
Spaghetti and Italian
 Meatballs, 110
Gumbo, Chicken with Smoked
 Sausage, 88

H

Halibut
 "Just for the Halibut"
  Burgers, 105
Ham
 Jambalaya, 107
 Pasta with Ham and
  Chicken Sauce, 108
 Wellington, 106
Hazelnut Cheesecake, 160
Herb
 Creamy Herb Sauce, 104
 Marinated Steak, 72
 Omelet, 96
Herbed Fishwiches, 101
Hickory BBQ
 Fish, 100
 Sauce, 100
High altitude, 182, 183
Hiker's or Biker's Birdseed, 154
Hoppin' John Jambalaya, 114
Horseradish Sauce, 126
Huevos Rancheros, 97
Humidity, 181

I

Insalata
 Caprese, 128
 Russa, 127
Irish Cream Cheesecake, 161
Italian
 Baked Cornish Hen, 90
 Baked Fish 99
 Breaded Fried Trout, 102
 Carrot Salad, 131

193

Cheeseball, 29
Meatballs, 110
Meatloaf, 109
Mustard Dressing, 132
Oven-Roasted Potatoes, 143
Roast Chicken, 79
Submarine Sandwich, 111
Tuna Salad, 123
Tuna-Egg Salad, 123
White Bean Soup, 122

J

"Just for the Halibut"
  Burgers, 105

K

Kabobs
  Beef, 68
  Chicken-Pepper, 84
Kahlúa Cheesecake, 161
Karol's Cinnamon Coffee, 41

L

Lemon-Butter Sauce, 135
Lemon-Dill Catfish, 100
Linzertorte, 172
Liptauer Cheese Spread, 29
Loading Your Camper/RV, 22-24
Louisiana Field Peas and
  Rice, 144
Low Country Clam Chowder, 116

M

Manhattan Clam Chowder, 120
Manicotti, 74
Marinated
  Roast Beef, 64
  Venison, 64
Maryland Crab Cakes, 92
Master Shopping/Supply List, 12
Mediterranean Rice, 144
Menus, 174-179
Metric Equivalents, 187
Mexican
  Cheeseball, 30

Hot Chocolate, 41
  Style Deviled Eggs, 37
Midwestern BBQ Sauce, 125
Milk Chocolate
  Cheesecake, 164
  Dipped Strawberries, 169
  Fondue, 168
Minestrone 118
Monterey Omelet, 96
Mousse
  Chocolate Amaretto, 170
  Chocolate Amaretto Pie, 170
  Creamy Lemon, 171
Muenster Dill Tart, 98
Mulled Cranberry-Port, 43
Mushroom-Almond Paté, 25
Mustard Butter Sauce, 101

N

Napolitano Tomato Sauce, 110
New England Clam Chowder, 116
New York Deli Pizza, 56
Nippy Cheese Canapés, 34
Northern Fried Chicken, 83
Nuts, see appetizers

O

Omelet, see eggs
Onion-Herb Stuffed
  Zucchini, 149
Onion Soup, 116
Orange Cheesecake, 159
Oranges Curaçao, 169
Oreo Cheesecake, 162

P

Pain Perdu, 94
Pancakes
  Apple, 54
  Pecan, 54
Parmesan Popcorn, 35
Pasta
  Frittata, 111
  with Ham and Chicken
    Sauce, 108
  Italian Tuna Salad, 123

Manicotti, 74
Ragù alla Bolognese, 114
Spaghetti all'
  Amatriciana, 61
Spaghetti alla
  Carbonara, 60
Spaghetti Salad, 128
with White Clam Sauce, 90
Paté, see appetizers
Peanut Butter
  Chippety Fudge, 154
  Cream of Peanut Soup, 119
  Truffles, 155
Peanut Sauce, 126
Peanuts, Cheesy Smoked, 36
Peas, Green
  Petit Pois aux Laitues, 142
Pecan
  Baked Chicken, 84
  Cookies, 157
  Pancakes, 54
  Rice, 146
  Spiced, 36
Petit Pois aux Laitues, 142
Pie
  Chocolate Amaretto
    Mousse, 170
  Chocolate Chip, 172
Pimiento Cheeseball, 30
Pineapple, French Brandied, 167
Pissaladière, 59
Pizza
  Cookie, 155
  New York Deli, 56
  Stromboli, 58
Pollo alla Forno, 80
Popcorn, Parmesan, 35
Pork Chops
  Sage with Green Pepper
    Sauce, 113
  Tuscany, 113
Potato
  Baked Potato Dumplings, 140
  Bean-Potato Burritos, 137
  Crocchette di Patate, 143
  Croquettes, 143
  Green Onion-Black Olive
    Salad, 130
  Italian Oven-Roasted, 143

Southwest Style
  Scalloped, 140
Praline Cheesecake, 161
Profiteroles, 166

Q

Quesadillas, 35
Quiche, Green Chili, 95
Quick Paté, 26

R

Ragù alla Bolognese, 114
Raisin-Raspberry Sauce, 92
Raisin Scones, 45
Red Cabbage, German Style, 138
Red Pepper Spread, 32
Refried Beans, see beans,
  refried
Rice
  Chicken Fried, 86
  Insalata Russa, 127
  Louisiana Field Peas and
    Rice, 144
  Mediterranean, 144
  Pecan, 146
  Risotto Milanese, 146
  Rojo, 145
  Spanish, 141
Risotto Milanese, 146
Roast Beef, see beef, roast
Roast Duck with Raisin-
  Raspberry Sauce, 92
Rojo Rice, 145
Rouladen, 62
Rum-Raisin Coffeecake, 52

S

Sage Pork Chops, 113
Salad Dressings
  Blue Cheese, 32
  Italian Mustard, 132
  Thousand Island, 132
Salads
  Antipasto, 132
  Beet Tossed, 134
  Bird of Paradise Chicken, 82

195

Broccoli-Cauliflower, 131
California Style Chicken, 82
Carrot, Italian Style, 131
Coleslaw
  Cream Slaw, 130
  Southern Style, 129
Creole Green Bean-Red
  Pepper, 129
Deli, 133
Green Onion-Black Olive
  Potato, 130
Insalata Caprese, 128
Insalata Russa, 127
Italian Tuna, 123
Italian Tuna-Egg, 123
Southern Ambrosia, 127
Spaghetti, 128
Spinach-Mushroom, 133
Zesty Steak, 70
Salmon
  Broiled with Creamy Herb
    Sauce, 104
  Broiled with Parmesan
    Topping, 103
  "Smoked" Salmon Spread, 33
Salsa, 31
Santa Fe Frappé, 40
Sauces
  Bagna Cauda, 31
  Caribbean BBQ, 125
  Cranberry-Amaretto, 124
  Creamy Herb, 104
  Creole, 66
  Creole Butter, 98
  Deluxe Tartar, 105
  Double-Bar Ranch BBQ, 78
  Easy
    Cheese, 137
    Tartar, 104
  Enchilada, 63
  Green Pepper, 32
  Hickory BBQ, 100
  Horseradish, 126
  Lemon Butter, 135
  Midwestern BBQ, 125
  Mustard Butter, 101
  Napolitano Tomato, 110
  Peanut, 126
  Ragù alla Bolognese, 114

Raisin-Raspberry, 92
  Salsa, 31
  Spanish, 102
  Super-Quick Sweet
    and Sour, 89
  Tartar, 104, 105
Sausage
  Hoppin' John Jambalaya, 114
  Ragù alla Bolognese, 114
Scaloppini alla Marsala, 124
Scones
  Cheese, 44
  Raisin, 45
Scrambled Eggs with Mush-
  room, 97
Shish Kabob
  Beef, 68
  Chicken-Pepper, 84
Shopping List
  Joyce Ryan's, 16
  Master, 12
Shrimp
  Creole, 115
  Log, 33
"Smoked" Salmon Spread, 33
Soup
  Borscht, 120
  Bouillabaisse, 121
  Chicken-Corn Chowder, 117
  Chicken Gumbo with Smoked
    Sausage, 88
  Crab Bisque, 118
  Cream of Peanut, 119
  Gazpacho, 122
  Italian White Bean
    Soup, 122
  Low Country Clam
    Chowder, 116
  Manhattan Clam Chowder, 120
  Minestrone, 118
  New England Clam Chowder, 116
  Onion Soup, 116
Southern
  Ambrosia, 127
  Coleslaw, 129
  Fried Chicken, 83
South-of-France Cornish Hen, 91
Southwest Style Scalloped
  Potatoes, 140

Spaghetti
  all'Amatriciana, 61
  alla Carbonara, 60
  and Italian Meatballs, 110
  Salad, 128
Spanish
  Rice, 141
  Sauce, 102
Spiced Pecans, 36
Spinach-Mushroom
  Casserole, 147
  Salad, 133
Spirited Cafe' Mocha, 41
Spreads, see appetizers
Steak, see beef
Steak Waikiki, 67
Stir-Fried Chicken
  with Broccoli, 85
  with Lettuce, 89
Strawberry
  Breakfast Cake, 53
  Daiquiris, 39
  Fans, 168
  Milk Chocolate Dipped, 169
Stromboli, 58
Substitutions, 184-186
Super-Quick Sweet and Sour
  Sauce, 89
Supply List
  Joyce Ryan's, 16
  Master, 12
Sweet
  "Rolls", 46
  Wheaty Biscuits, 44
Syrup, Blueberry, 54

T

Taramosalata, 28
Tartar Sauce
  Deluxe, 105
  Easy, 104
Teriyaki Steak, 67
Thousand Island Dressing, 132
Toffee Fudge, 153
Trout, Italian-Breaded
  Fried, 102
Tuna
  Italian Tuna Salad, 123

Italian Tuna-Egg Salad, 123
Turkey sausage
  Ragù alla Bolognese, 114

U

Uova 'mpriatorio, 95

V

Veal
  Scaloppini alla Marsala, 124
Velvet Hammer Frappé, 40
Venison, Marinated Roast, 64

W

Walnuts, Cheesy Smoked, 36
Western
  Baked Beans, 136
  Omelet, 96
White Chocolate
  Cheesecake, 163
White Clam Sauce, 90
Wholesome Wheat Beer
  Bread, 50
Wurst Bites, 37

Y

Yorkshire Pudding, 55

Z

Zesty Steak Salad, 70
Zippy BBQ Steak, 72
Zucchini
  Julienne, 148
  Onion-Herb Stuffed, 149
  with Sour Cream
    Topping, 148

About the Author

Joyce Ryan is an expert cook as well as an author, artist, and experienced traveler. Her books include: TRAVELING WITH YOUR SKETCHBOOK, SEOUL TRAVEL GUIDE, SCENES OF SOUTHERN ARIZONA, and SEOUL SKETCHES. She has exhibited extensively in the United States and abroad. Listed in Who's Who, her drawings are in private collections throughout the United States, Europe, Japan, and Korea.

**BUTTERFLY
B O O K S**

4210 Misty Glade
San Antonio, Texas 78247

ORDER FORM

**Please send me ___ copies of The Happy Camper's
Gourmet Cookbook @ $11.95 each.**

Total amount for books:	$ _____
$2.00 for postage/handling	$ _____
Texas residents add 8% sales tax (96¢ for 1 book)	$ _____
Total amount enclosed:	$ _____

Please make check payable to BUTTERFLY BOOKS.

Mail book(s) to:

Name:_____

Address:_____

City:_____

State/Zip:_____

Thank you for your order!